Daily Boosts

365

Motivation for the Mind

Robert Herdman

Copyright © 2016 Robert Herdman

All rights reserved.

ISBN:1534719709

ISBN-13:9781534719705

Table of Contents

Dedication v

Acknowledgments vii

Foreword ix

Introduction 1

How to Use This Book. 7

Daily Boosts 365 9

Author's Note 205

Dedication

To everyone who has faced

Adversity in life and has picked themselves up, dusted themselves off and just got on with it.

To those out there who are struggling with life at the moment; things are never as bad as they seem in the moment.

A renewed mind is a healthy mind and a healthy mind is the start of a new life.

Acknowledgments

I want to thank:

All the people I have mentioned in the pages throughout this book that have given such great quotes, metaphors and stories throughout history. These bits of wisdom are not only timeless, but when read, have the power to turn a person's life around in an instant.

Sean Connolly, for taking the time to write the foreword of this book. A good friend and fellow coach.

Adian Hughes, for once again taking the time to go through the editing process and bringing the content up to scratch grammatically. (Just 7 more books to go).

Foreword

I first met Robert twenty years ago at my mind/body clinic where he came for a muscle strain. A former Irish Champion bodybuilder, he was also running a couple of businesses at the time. He noticed one of my Hypnotherapy certificates hanging on the wall and asked me about the theory behind hypnosis and had I ever heard of N.L.P. (Neuro Linguistic programming). On Robert's next visit he turned up with a box of books and cassette tapes, all on the subject of NLP and said, "There you are, when you have finished with them I will bring you some more." Needless to say Robert went on to train and qualify in Hypnosis with many of the top teachers in the world and is still as enthusiastic today about his profession in helping to change other people's lives as he was back then. The word procrastination has been ripped out from Robert's dictionary in life. Still an avid reader on the subject of personal development he has started the process of writing his own books, expressing his knowledge and his own unique methods for human development. Robert's burning passion for his work is something that is unique and it comes across in the pages of his books. I am sure you will feel some of that passion yourself as you turn through the pages. I have known Robert for just over twenty years and I can honestly say the content of his work comes from his heart. His "no excuses" approach, both his own life and working with clients have set him up as one of the most sought after Mind Coaches in Ireland over the last ten years. He has literally work with thousands of clients over the last ten years and I can truly say he is a coach that comes from a background of vast experience, working with client in business, sport, and therapy through his busy private practice. This book does exactly what it says on the tin; offers you daily bite-sized chunks of motivation and inspiration that will act as a "pick me up" when you need it. A great wee book that I know will be a huge success to all those looking continued personal development.

Sean Connolly

Author of "The little book of Inspirations for Irish Dancing"

"Dancing Minds: Secrets from the Masters"

Introduction

This book is a bit different from most books. It's not a novel, nor is it to be read as a novel. I consider "Daily Boosts365" as a pick me up, to be used as a source of motivation and inspiration on a daily basis.

There is no right or wrong way to read through it. There are no chapters or contents page but it is set out in a very specific way.

Let me explain!

As we go through life we never know what faces us from one day to the next.

Many times, even though we may have a plan that we're working towards, stuff just happens. We are faced with a situation that we didn't expect; people react in ways that surprise us or life presents us with a problem that wasn't on the menu. Loved ones pass suddenly, relationships break down, so called friends do the unexpected, the list is endless.

In my first book "The Success Habit: A Journey to Self-Mastery, I talk about the process of renewing the mind and how important it is for our mental wellbeing.

I believe that what happens to us, even dramatic things like bankruptcy, divorce, death or even economic recession cannot directly cause a feeling of any kind until the brain interprets and creates a mental story about set situations. Sadness, depression, frustration, upset and anxiety can only be produced by seeing a certain situation and then producing an interpretation of it, then believing that interpretation. So therefore you and I can only be overwhelmed about our thoughts about something; never the things itself. So I believe it is important to go through a process of continuously renewing our minds on a daily basis; putting new ideas into our mind that creates a feel good factor and by the process of compounding and repetition reinforcing those ideas so that we naturally feel better.

I also believe there is a correct way to get the full benefits from the process.

Most people wait until they are challenged by life and hit rock bottom or face a feeling of total overwhelm or hopelessness before they would ever think of picking up a self-help book. But think about the last time you felt really down or felt depressed and someone said to you, "Cheer up, it's going to be ok" or "Things are not as bad as they seem, it will get better." How many times did that work or help you feel better? Probably none! You were in that negative mindset and everything within your nervous system was telling you that things were bad. The way you were using your physiology, the language you were using inside your mind and what you were focusing on to reinforce the bad feeling. Then someone comes along with a suggestion to help you feel better but because your neurology was in total contradiction to that suggestion, then it was totally rejected by the conscious mind.

That controlling voice inside your head was saying; "What do you know?" "If you only knew how I was feeling!" "Oh it's ok for you, if you had to live my life you wouldn't be so positive."

I believe the best time to put new ideas into your mind is when you feel good. When you are in top form and things are going the way you want, your mind is very open to positive suggestion.

If you take the same scenario where someone comes up to you and says something like, "You look great," "Things are starting to look up for you," Well done, you're a true inspiration," because you are in the positive vibration that voice inside your head is saying, "Course I am," "Why would I not be?" "I know and it feels great!"

The thing about life is this! When we are born we come into the world in a natural state of wellbeing. Babies don't get depressed, stressed or anxious. They are trained to become that way through the process of life.

When we are born we are not give an owner's manual for our brain that shows us how to respond when we feel mentally challenged. So we become conditioned into our primary emotional state by the continuous process of how we react to life's situations.

When we are faced with a situation in life, there is an emotional content that comes along with that experience. Even though the experience comes and goes, the emotional content is stored at a Sub-Conscious level and can be accessed through our memory recall. When we face future situations of a similar nature we go through a process of "emotional resonance." The mind resonates back to the last experience and the feeling now becomes stronger.

We then link certain feelings and emotions with certain situations and this becomes habit.

But the point I'm trying to make is that we train ourselves to do this, through a process of repetition.

Now, as a child growing up, we may not have the ability to recognise and control this process, but as adults we do.

When you take the time, you can train your mind to do almost anything.

What we allow into our minds on a daily basis will contribute to how we feel on a daily basis and how we feel on a daily basis will determine how we behave on a daily basis.

So if you go through the process of renewing your mind

daily then you are reinforcing the feel good factor you experience each day.

Now am I saying that when you start renewing your mind, you're never going to have a bad day? No I'm not. But you're not going to live in that mindset on a daily basis and you will find that the "bad days" will come less often.

How to Use This Book.

Just as you can never tell what is going to happen in life each day, you can never always determine the things that make you feel better each day. Sometimes you are faced with a problem that you have made so big in your mind and something really simple makes you feel better instantly without no effort at all on your part. The smile of a baby, a simple quote you read, a story of someone else's success or a pet doing something hilarious that made you totally forgot what it is you were feeling down about. You got that instant "pick me up."

This book is to be used in the same way. It can be read from cover to cover but I recommend the best way to use it, is it to simply flick through and just open it at whatever page you stop at and presuppose that whatever message you read is going to be the right one for you at the time.

This book has 365 separate pieces of information contained within its cover. There are simple quotes, poems and inspirational and motivational stories that are there to help you feel better. They are in no specific order and, as I said, are not separated into chapters.

They are combined together so that as you flick through the book and stop at a random page, you're getting something different. But the theme of the book is to help to motivate, so each quote, poems and story has been hand pick by me, as I know they work. I have been using them for over ten years and over that period, I have been writing them down. Over a ten-year period I accumulated a series of journals that comprised of great information that has helped me develop my mindset so I decided to put them together and this collection is the result.

The pieces of information throughout the content of this book are from famous people from history, from simple stories with a moral, inspirational successes from ordinary people who achieved massive results and some things that I have personally written myself. I have not put them in a specific order but instead decided to randomly place them through the pages so that they could be read at any time and in any order. So, I have accredited each quotes and story with that specific authors name at the bottom of each so that you know who wrote what. If it doesn't have a name after, then it has been written by myself.

So I hope you take pleasure in this collection of quotes, poems and short stories.

As you flick through the pages I hope you make this part of your daily routine as you never know, it could be one of these simple pieces of information throughout this book that could turn your day around.

Enjoy.

Daily Boosts 365

1.

Obstacles can't stop you.

Problems can't stop you.

Most of all, other people can't stop you.

Only You Can Stop You.

(Jeoffrey Gitomer)

2.

Personal Development always works but only when used as it should be. It works when we understand that it's about personal transformation and not about "get rich quick" gimmicks or slick techniques to influence people. Personal Development is about changing the way we see the world. It's about developing yourself as a person. It's about changing our pattern of thinking, about changing what we choose to focus on and mostly about changing our fundamental attitude. When you want to change any area of your life you have to start with changing yourself. The thing that is missing when people want to change any area in their lives is Discipline, Commitment, Persistence, Diligence and getting back up when you have a set back and starting all over again, instead of giving up and blaming other people or your circumstances. It's amazing the things that start to happen around you when you take the time and change your world from the inside out, developing some "Stick ability" in your life. "The World is Your Oyster." It's up to you to make things happen. When you get on board and are committed to following through; whatever personal development program you decide to follow works just fine.

3.

You may not be where you want to be right now,

But that's nothing to do with your future.

(Zig Ziglar)

4.

Quitting Is Not The Way

Go ahead and quit,
If you can't see it through.
But don't come crying to me,
When quitting is all you do.

Those who start to quit,
When things start getting tough.
Start to see quitting,
As a way to get out of stuff.

Robert Herdman

They never stick things through,
And can't complete a thing.
Is this the type of person,
You see yourself being?

Quitters never win,
No matter what you've heard.
Have you ever heard a quitter,
That is picked to be referred?

Of course that would be silly,
Why would someone refer?
Someone who can't even accomplish,
They are their own saboteurs.

Next time you want to quit,
Think who you want to be.
Quitters never win,
I want more than this for thee.

I want to see success,
Surround you every day.
I want you to be happy,
And want to scream hooray!

I want you in a job,
That makes you're world so good.
I want the work you do,
Feel just like childhood.

But most of all I want,
To see you see things through.
But not because you should,
Because you really want too.

And I realise you may be scared,
That you can't see it through.
But I'm here to tell you, you can,
Do anything you put your mind to.

(Julie Herbert)

5.

A POUND OF BUTTER

There was a farmer who sold a pound of butter to the baker. One day the baker decided to weigh the butter to see if he was getting a pound and he found that he was not. This angered him and he took the farmer to court. The Judge asked the farmer if he was using any measure? The farmer replied, "No Your Honor, I am primitive. I don't have a proper measure, but I do have a scale." The

Judge asked, "Then how do you weigh the butter?" The farmer replied "Your Honor, long before the baker started buying butter from me, I have been buying a pound loaf of bread from him. Every day when the baker brings the bread, I put it on the scale and give him the same weight in butter. If anyone is to be blamed, it is the baker."

What is the moral of the story? We get back in life what we give to others. Whenever you take an action, ask yourself this question; Am I giving fair value for the wages or money I hope to make? Honesty and dishonesty become a habit. Some people practice dishonesty and can lie with a straight face. Others lie so much that they don't even know what the truth is anymore. But who are they deceiving? Themselves.

(Anonymous)

6.

When you have lived your life and you reflect on your journey, will you remember all the amazing things you have achieved because you overcame the challenges along the way, took continuous action and lived life to the full?

Or will you think about all the regrets you have because you put things off, spent each year making excuses and let other people's opinion control your life?

It's never too late to take back control of your life.

7.

The best day of your life is the one on which you decide your life is your own;

No Apologies; No Excuses

No one to lean on, rely on or blame.

The gift is yours-

It is an amazing journey-

And you alone are responsible for the quality of it.

This is the day your life really begins

(Bob Moawad)

8.

The Stonecutter and the Angel

Once upon a time there was a young stonecutter who looked with envy upon the rich merchant who employed him. One day he was muttering to himself about what it would be like to have such freedom and power when, to his amazement, an angel appeared and spoke the words "You are what you have said." In an instant, the stonecutter had become the merchant.

He was very happy with his lot until he saw the king of the land ride by with his coterie. "Now that's the way to live," he thought. Almost before he had asked, the angel had granted his wish and the merchant had become the king.

All was well until one beautiful summer's day when the king began sweating in his heavy royal garb. "What freedom and power the sun has," he thought. "It can float through the sky and call forth water from a king. That is what I would truly like to be."

As the thought appeared in his mind, the angel appeared to grant it.

Now the king had become the sun, and he reveled in his freedom and power as he floated high above the earth. But after a time, a cloud appeared and blocked the land from his view. When he watched the lightning burst forth from the cloud and heard the roar of the thunder, he knew that he was witnessing true freedom and power. Before he even realised what was happening, the angel had transformed him into a cloud.

What fun it was to pour rain forth upon the land! Wherever the man-cloud went, forests were washed away, and puddles became oceans in his wake. But no matter how hard he tried, there was one huge mountain made of stone that stood immovable and unaffected by his rain.

"Surely that is the ultimate power," he thought. "To stand tall in the face of any circumstance—that is true freedom and power."

In an instant, the angel had made it so, and the man could feel the incredible power of being an immovable object in the midst of any storm. Yet even as he was delighting in his immense strength and resilience, he could see a small man chipping away at his base with a pick and a chisel and a hammer.

"That man is even more powerful than I," he thought. "See how he is able to take stone away from me with just a few blows of his mighty tools. That is the kind of freedom and power I have always longed for."

The angel appeared and once again spoke the words "You are what you have said."

And with those words, the older but wiser stonecutter continued on his journey.

(Adapted from a Japanese folk tale)

9.

Success is based on right thinking;

Failure is based on wrong thinking

And your life will be based on

The Way You Think

10.

Our greatest weakness lies in giving up.

The most certain way to succeed is always to try just one more time.
(Thomas Edison)

11.

How many times have you let other people's opinion stop you from trying something you really wanted to do? People are always going to have their opinions, even their opinions of you. When your focus is on creating your own future, then these opinions don't matter. Make the decision to let go of what doesn't matter and the opinions of the "nay sayers."

Let it go so you can grow into the person you need to become, to be successful at whatever it is you are wanting to achieve.

Being successful at anything is all about you and when you get "YOU" right, then nothing or no-one can stop you from achieving what it is you want to achieve. Focus on getting yourself right and amazing things will happen in your life.

12.

Positive thought for Today

When you feel that nobody loves you,

Nobody cares about you,

Everyone is ignoring you

And people are jealous of you.

You should ask yourself....

Am I Too SEXY?

13.

There comes a time in life when you must make the difficult decision to let certain things go; a negative attitude or bad habit that you know no longer serves you; a relationship where you are dying together as opposed to growing together; an addiction that you know is destroying you and does not represent your true self.

It takes courage to face the truth about who you are, the choices that you have been making in your life and to decide; that is just not me anymore. I cannot do this anymore. I have had it.

It takes a level of self-love, dedication and determination to live your greatest life. So, look within. Look at every area of your life and ask yourself these questions; Am I on course? Am I growing mentally, emotionally and spiritually? Is there anything that is preventing me from living my greatest life? Make the tough decision to let it go. Life is about surrendering and releasing. Surrendering to the higher calling of your life and releasing all of the things, habits and behaviours that no longer serve you.

Bad habits, bad relationships, bad choices and decisions stop us from being the person we can truly be. We are only ever one decision away from turning things around in your life. That decision has to come from YOU. No-one else can make it for you.

14.

Logic will get you from A to B.

Imagination will take you everywhere.

(Albert Einstein)

15.

Other people's opinion of you is none of your business;

So why would you get emotionally involved?

Focus on what you can control,

Not what you have no control over.

15.

The Triple-Filter Test

In Ancient Greece, Socrates was reputed to hold knowledge in high esteem. One day an acquaintance met the great philosopher and said, "Do you know what I just heard about your friend?"

"Hold on a minute," Socrates replied. "Before you talk to me about my friend, it might be good idea to take a moment and filter what you're going to say. That's why I call it the triple filter test. The first filter is Truth. Have you made absolutely sure that what you are about to tell me is true?"

"Well, no," the man said, "actually I just heard about it and…"

"All right," said Socrates. "So you don't really know if it's true or not. Now, let's try the second filter, the filter of

Goodness. Is what you are about to tell me about my friend something good?"

"Umm, no, on the contrary…"

"So," Socrates continued, "you want to tell me something bad about my friend, but you're not certain it's true. You may still pass the test though, because there's one filter left—the filter of Usefulness. Is what you want to tell me about my friend going to be useful to me?"

"No, not really."

"Well," concluded Socrates, "if what you want to tell me is neither true, nor good, nor even useful, why tell it to me at all?"

16.

Many people want to change different parts of their lives; Become slimmer, stop smoking, become financially independent, it's different for each individual. Yet it's only around 2% of the people who actually realise they have to change before the change happens. The other 98% are so focused on the diet, the nicotine patches, the money making ideas, that they never realise it is themselves they need to change to achieve the results.

"TO CHANGE YOUR LIFE YOU NEED TO CHANGE YOUR LIFE."

This may seem a play on words but it's not. You need to develop the mindset of a slimmer person to stay slim permanently.

You need to develop the mindset of a rich person to accumulate any significant money in your life and keep it. You need to develop the mindset of a non-smoker to become and stay a non-smoker for the rest of your life. Developing the mindset of the person you want to become, along the way to your goal, is more important than the goal itself. Renewing your mind is an essential ingredient in your journey to being successful. When you commit to developing yourself mentally on a daily basis, things on the outside world change in accordance with the new mindset.

17.

You are more than you think.

Be your own "Super Hero"

And watch what you can achieve.

18.

In my profession I meet a lot of what I call "Successful Victims;" People who blame circumstances, their past, their parents, their upbringing etc for not being where they want to be in life.

They have their story of why it's not their fault and it's all to do with everything on the outside.

We are creating our experience of life right now, moment by moment.

You always tend to see whatever it is you are looking for. When you act as if your experience is created from the outside in, you will experience yourself as a victim. The minute you take responsibility for creating your experience from the inside out; you reclaim your position as the creator of your life and therefore can go about changing it.

We all have the choice to proceed one way or the other. Are you a victim or a creator? Have an amazing day whichever one you decide to be.

19.

And suddenly you know;

It's time to start something new and trust the magic of new beginnings.

(Meister Eckhart)

20.

There is an old Cherokee Indian story about a tribal elder, who is teaching his grandson about life: "A fight is going on inside me," he says to the boy. "It's a terrible fight and is between two wolves. One is destructive; he represents anger, sorrow, regret, guilt, depression, fear, greed, arrogance, self-pity, resentment, inferiority, lies, false pride, superiority and ego. The other is good; he is joy, peace, love, hope, serenity, humility, kindness, happiness, empathy, generosity, truth, compassion and faith.

The same fight is going on inside of you and every other person to," he says to the boy.

The grandson thinks for a moment and then asks his grandfather, "Which wolf will win?"

The old Cherokee simply replies, "Whichever one you feed the most"

So as you read through this let me ask you a question: What are you feeding into you mind on a daily basis at this present time?

Is it constructive or destructive?

How are you making yourself feel each and every day? You are there twenty four hours a day, seven days a week, three hundred and sixty five days a year and you and you alone have the power to make yourself feel successful, amazing, happy or something entirely different.

21.

We all have the ability to succeed in life. We all have the ability to overcome those obstacles that life throws at us. We all have the ability to create a better life for ourselves and our loved ones. We all have a goal or dream that we want to achieve, whether we are still striving to achieve it or whether it is put to the back of our minds. I challenge everyone who reads this to start again. Find that dream and start your journey to fulfil that dream. The best way to predict your future is to create it yourself. We all have the ability to create our own future. Don't let the fear of the time it will take to accomplish something stand in the way of you doing it. The time will pass anyway, we may as well put that time to the best possible use. Where the heart is willing, it will find a thousand ways to accomplish your dream. If it is not, you will find a thousand excuses. Just go out there and do what you have to do, and never ever give up!

22.

You are the only problem in your life;

So, you are the only solution.

23.

One thing entrepreneurs should understand is the meaning of being an entrepreneur. An entrepreneur is someone who has chosen to do what he wants with his life. When you're doing what you want with your life, that is the greatest joy that you can have. But slowly, you forget that you are doing what you want. You start working for somebody else's expectations. That's not the way. The meaning of being an entrepreneur is that you are doing what you want to do. You should continue to do that all your life. Success is not only in terms of size. Success must also be looked at in terms of finding full expression of who you are, your capabilities and your competence. If any human being finds full expression of who he is, he will find success. If you compare yourself to somebody in another completely different area or arena of activity and put the numbers together, those numbers may be bigger – that's not the point. In your area of life, finding full expression is success.

The meaning of being an entrepreneur is that you are doing what you want to do and you should continue to do that all of your life.

So there is no need to be pressured by peer groups, media, this and that, as long as you are able to find full expression to who you are through the work that you're doing, and above all, establish your way of being. An entrepreneur does something that he cares for, that he wants to do. So it matters to him. His work is important. Once your work is important, the most important thing is, you must work upon yourself. This is completely missing. Managing a business essentially means you are managing other people and other people's minds. If you can't manage yours, how will you manage theirs? If you manage yours, where is the question of pressure? Where is the question of stress? There is no such thing. Work is not pressure. Work is not stress. It is your inability to manage yourself which is the stress.

Most people think it is their job, their family, their life situations, the taxes and the unpaid bills that are causing stress. But essentially, stress is your inability to manage your own system – your body, mind, emotions, and energy.

Stress is like friction in a machine. In other words, there is not enough lubrication in the system to function smoothly and easily. In everyone's life, situations occur, but each person manages them differently, depending upon how smoothly his or her own system functions within itself. If you know how to manage this human mechanism, there is no question of stress. How successful you are in the world essentially depends on how friction-free your own mechanism is. You can bring your system to a frictionless state of function with simple practices. An ongoing personal development program is essential to establish balance within yourself so that you can give full attention to your business and everyone around you.

24.

To be a winner in life you need to start talking and acting like a winner. You've got to start training your mind by programming success into it on a regular basis, so that the attitude of success comes out automatically.

25.

Shake off Your Problems

A man's favourite donkey falls into a deep precipice. He can't pull it out no matter how hard he tries. He therefore decides to bury it alive.

Soil is poured onto the donkey from above. The donkey feels the load, shakes it off, and steps on it. More soil is poured.

It shakes it off and steps up. The more the load was poured, the higher it rose. By noon, the donkey was grazing in green pastures.

After much shaking off (of problems) and stepping up (learning from them), one will graze in green pastures.

26.

There is no elevator to Success;

You have to take the stairs.

27.

Approval Seeking is one of the major things that stops people from growing in life. Looking for your value in the approval of others. Making another person's opinion of you more important that your own opinion of yourself. This is exactly what you do every single time you find yourself upset, depressed, out of sorts, even unhappy with the way someone has treated you or behaved towards you. When you experience these emotions as a result of how other people have treated you, what you are really saying is, "what that person thinks of me is more important than what I think of myself." People are going to dissapprove of you and others will even dislike you, but that's just part of life. Everyone is entitled to their own opinions and even their opinions of you. Learn to accept disapproval as part of life, even expect it 50% of the time. If you need someone's approval that means you are immobilised without it. When you expect disapproval then you're not surprised or immobilised when you get it. You have a choice. When someone says something to you that you dislike or behaves towards you in a way that you find offensive, you have a choice in how you process that. You must not turn the controls of your life over to someone else in the form of approval seeking. Accept disapproval and let the emotional content go in your mind. You'll be amazed how different you are around people when you don't need their approval.

28.

Take the whole responsibility on your shoulders,

Know that you are the creator of your own destiny.

All the strength and success you want is within yourself.

Stand up. Be bold. Be strong.

Make your Own future.

29.

What you focus on consistently is what you manifest in your life; No Exceptions. If you're focused on the negative, there could be all sorts of positive things and opportunities happening right before your very eyes and you don't even notice.

If you focus on the problem, there could be a solution right in front of you and you walk right pass it not even seeing it because, as obvious as that solution may be, if you get too focused in the wrong direction, it can actually blind you to certain realities. Start focusing on where you want to go in life not where you've been. You can't change the past but there is an amazing future out there waiting for you. Ask yourself these questions; What do I really want to happen in my life? What is stopping me from moving in that direction? What could I do from this moment forward that will start taking me in the right direction? By letting your mind meditate on the last question you have already started to shift your focus.

30.

Change Your World

You cannot change the world,
But you can present the world with one improved person -
Yourself.
You can go to work on yourself to make yourself
Into the kind of person you admire and respect.
You can become a role model and set a standard for others.
You can control and discipline yourself to resist acting
Or speaking in a negative way
Toward anyone for any reason.
You can insist upon always doing things the loving way,
Rather than the hurtful way.

By doing these things each day,
You can continue on your journey
Toward becoming an exceptional human being.

(Brian Tracy)

31.

GIVE YOURSELF A BIG HUG TODAY

A lot of people who come to see me have nothing wrong with them except for their thoughts getting in the way. The words we speak to ourselves in the privacy of our own minds have a direct effect upon our thoughts. The words we use help to condition and create our attitudes. The sub-conscious mind can take the things we say to ourselves literally. Be kinder to yourself and start using words that will stimulate the feelings of confidence, happiness and joy. When was the last time you complimented yourself and gave yourself an emotional HUG by telling yourself how great you are......The words we use determine how we think. How we think determines how we feel. How we feel determines our attitudes. Our attitudes determine what actions we will take in life. Our actions ultimately take us in a specific direction each and every day. If you end up depressed, fearful, anxious or stressed each day; it's not an accident. It's a result of what you have been programming into your mind over a period of time. Start over. Start by changing what you are saying to yourself each day. Give yourself an emotional hug by reminding yourself of all the good qualities that are within you.

32.

Change your world

By changing what's going on in your mind.

33.

BANK ACCOUNT

Imagine there is a bank, which credits your account each morning with £86,400, carries over no balance from day to day, allows you to keep no cash balance and every evening cancels whatever part of the amount you had failed to use during the day. What would you do? Draw out every pound, of course!

Everyone has such a bank. It's name is Time.

Every morning, it credits you with 86,400 seconds. Every night it writes off, as lost, whatever of this you have failed to invest to good purpose. It carries over no balance. It allows no overdraft. Each day it opens a new account for you. Each night it burns the records of the day. If you fail to use the day's deposits, the loss is yours.

There is no going back. There is no drawing against the "tomorrow."

Therefore, there is never not enough time or too much time. Time management is decided by us alone and nobody else. It is never the case of us not having enough time to do things, but the case of whether we want to do it.

34.

A relationship with another person is supposed to be an amazing experience. Sharing your life together and building a future full of love, excitement, uncertainty and excitement in the unknown. You build character, you develop each other along the way and you build and create a bond that is unstoppable. But when you go into a relationship and bring your past relationship experiences with you, you are missing so much of what could be. You hold back, you sometimes expect the same things to happen as before, you miss out on that MAGIC that should be. Let go of the past, it's over, you have already paid the price. You don't have to keep paying for it over and over in your mind every day. When you meet someone who you think could be the right person; jump in with both feet and watch that MAGIC happen. You're gonna make mistakes and get it wrong from time to time, but that's just part of being human. If you love someone and they love you, then you get through the obstacles and move forward, no matter what. Look at the future and create whatever you want, without looking back at what has happened before. There is an amazing life out there for you with the right person. GO MAKE IT HAPPEN.

35.

A man is but a product of his thoughts;

What he thinks, he becomes.

(Gandhi)

36.

I choose….

to live by choice, not by chance;

to make changes, not excuses;

to be useful, not used;

to excel, not compete;

I Choose Self-Esteem, not self-pity.

I choose to listen to my

inner voice,

not the random opinions of others.

37.

In theory making decisions should be one of the easiest things in the world for us to do. After all, we either want to do something or we don't. So why is decision making so difficult so much of the time? Mostly because we get caught up in our thoughts that the decision matters and that in some way we could or should know in advance how things will turn out. What you decide will never impact your life as much as how you handle the consequences of that decision. Example: Marrying the wrong person is just a mistake, staying married to them for the next 10 years and being miserable about it, is a bad decision. Making mistakes in life is part of the process. What can make things easier is by recognizing that no matter what you decide, you can almost always change your mind. Feeling guilt about your decisions is simply a futile exercise because it stops you from experiencing the amazing future you have in front of you. There is no right or wrong. When you let go of trying to get it right, you already know what to do. You know who you are.

38.

If you want to become successful at anything in life and haven't already achieved it, then the only question you should be asking yourself right now is:

"WHAT AM I GOING TO DO ABOUT IT?"

This one question will direct your mind in the direction necessary to take the next step.

Thinking about why you are not successful, will not get you there.

Blaming other people for not being successful, will not get you there.

Putting things off until tomorrow or Monday, will not get you there

The 101 excuses you have used before, will not get you there.

Ask yourself these two questions:

What do I really want to achieve in my life RIGHT NOW ?

So, what am I going to do about it RIGHT NOW?

When you answer the second question honestly then you will know what the next step will be.

It's up to you to take that next step and until you do you're going to stay right where you are.

Becoming successful in life is a lot simpler than you think; It's really all about "YOU" getting involved.

39.

The Man in the Glass

When you get what you want in your struggle for self
And the world makes you king for a day.
Just go to the mirror and look at yourself
And see what that man has to say.

For it isn't your father, or mother, or wife
Whose judgment upon you must pass.
The fellow whose verdict counts most in your life
Is the one staring back from the glass.

He's the fellow to please – never mind all the rest
For he's with you, clear to the end.
And you've passed your most difficult, dangerous test
If the man in the glass is your friend.

You may fool the whole world down the pathway of years
And get pats on the back as you pass.
But your final reward will be heartache and tears
If you've cheated the man in the glass.

(Peter Dale Wimbrow)

40.

Confidence to your mind is like the fuel of a car. You won't go where you want to go in life without confidence. When you set a goal, you don't see it happening straight away but you have to have the confidence that your payday will come.

41.

Champions aren't made in the gym.

Champions are made from something they have deep inside them.

A desire; a dream; a vision

They have to have the skill and the will.

But the will must be much stronger than the skill

(Muhammad Ali)

42.

We all want success in life and success to each of us means something totally different, but very few of us are willing to pay the price of success. There is a process to follow and people usually have problems with the process. Failure on the other hand, no matter what you want in life, can only be described in one way. Failure is man's inability to reach his goals in life, whatever they may be. The thing about life is that there is no failure unless you give up and stop trying. Every attempt brings with it an experience and we always get feedback from that experience. If it is not the result we want, then we can choose to give up or re-adjust our attitude or thinking and learn from our experiences and move forward. There is no failure; just feedback and every piece of feedback brings with it the chance to learn, develop and progress in life. People talk about success but are really looking for a quick fix. They tend to live in a microwave world. They want it yesterday. The thing about success is this; the process of success is the small steps each and every day, dealing with the obstacles and problems, being knocked down and getting up one more time and each time learning from what hasn't worked and adjusting your sails to progress in a new direction until you eventually succeed. And out of all this you develop your character and become someone who is successful from the inside out.

43.

Motivation is what gets you started;

Habit is what keeps you going.

(Brain Tracy)

44.

What did you what to be or do with your life when you were a child? Are you living that dream now? If you're not, what limiting beliefs are stopping you from really being what you what to be? Reignite that passion inside of you again and start creating who you really want to be. We all have the ability to change our circumstances and life no matter how hard it seems at the minute; No exceptions.

45.

The Five D's of being successful at anything in life.

1. DECISION: You have to make a true decision of what it is you want. A true decision is not giving it a try, it's you deciding on a specific goal and cutting off any possibility that you will not achieve it. You decide to succeed, no matter what.

2. DESIRE: You have to have a desire for what it is you want to achieve. When your desire for chocolate is stronger than your desire for weight loss, you will always give into your desire. But when you desire to become slimmer, healthier and your ideal weight, is greater than overeating, then you will overcome the challenges along the way.

3. DETERMINATION: Along the way to any goal

there are always going to be challenges and temptations. This is when that determination to succeed will over-ride the setbacks. Every successful person faces challenges and setbacks, but one commonality that set them apart is the determination to succeed.

4. DISCIPLINE: Success is about doing the right things, day after day after day. It's about getting up each morning and living by a set of rituals and carrying out those rituals until the day ends and then getting up the next day and repeating the process, whether you feel like it or not.

5. DEDICATION: Being loyal to your goal and following through to it's achievement is a test of how dedicated you are to actually achieving that goal.

Achieving any goal in life is about putting in the simple things each day, mentally and physically, until they become habit. People have the tendency to give up easily, not because they can't achieve their goal but because they lost some or all of the above qualities. It's easier to give up; it's easier to blame other people or circumstances. No matter what way you cut it, everyone has the ability to accomplish any goal they set out to achieve. The key is to take it one day at a time and retrain their nervous system, developing the confidence and new found belief along the way.

46.

No matter how far away your goal may seem,

the next step in reaching that goal is right in front of you.

The only step that matters right now is the next step.

Ask yourself the question,

"What's the next step I need to take right now that will bring me closer to my goal?"

And then take it.

47.

As human beings we are all choice making individuals and when we are faced with situations daily, we have a choice as to which direction to take. At any time in your life you can choose to stop doing something that is not working and make a new choice to do something different instead, that will lead you in a new direction. I'm sure as you read this you can think back to a decision you made years ago that if you had of made a different decision back then would have taken you in a different direction to the point where your life would have turned out differently now.

Today is no different. Today, as you reading this, could be a major breakthrough because you made a decision to take responsibility for your life in a certain area and also decided no longer to blame other people or circumstances or your past.

Where you are in life right now at this present time, is no one else's fault. You are where you are because of the decisions and choices you made in the past. Where you will end up in five years and ten years' time, will depend on the decisions and the choices you make right now at this stage of your life.

Just because you have been going through that behavior for five year or ten years or even twenty years, doesn't mean you can't learn to do something different. For things to change in your life, you have to change. And that takes some effort on your part.

Five years from now, ten years from now, you are going to arrive somewhere. The question is, where? Now is the time to fix the next ten years of your life.

48.

By changing your thinking,
You change your beliefs;

When you change your beliefs,
You change your expectations;

When you change your expectations,
You change your attitude;

When you change your attitude,
You change your behavior;

When you change your behavior,
You change your performance;

When you change your performance;
You change your Life!

(unknown)

49.

A bad attitude is like a flat tire,

You can't go anywhere until you change it.

(Robert Herdman)

50.

The Butterfly

A man found a cocoon of a butterfly. One day a small opening appeared. He sat and watched the butterfly for several hours as it struggled to force its body through that little hole. Then it seemed to stop making any progress. It appeared as if it had gotten as far as it could and it could go no further.

So the man decided to help the butterfly. He took a pair of scissors and snipped off the remaining bit of the cocoon. The butterfly then emerged easily but it had a swollen body and small, shrivelled wings.

The man continued to watch the butterfly because he expected that, at any moment, the wings would enlarge and expand to be able to support the body, which would contract in time. Neither happened! In fact, the butterfly spent the rest of it's life crawling around with a swollen body and shrivelled wings. It never was able to fly.

What the man, in his kindness and haste, did not understand, was that the restricting cocoon and the struggle required for the butterfly to get through the tiny opening were God's way of forcing fluid from the body of the butterfly into it's wings so that it would be ready for flight once it achieved it's freedom from the cocoon.

Sometimes struggles are exactly what we need in our lives. If God allowed us to go through our lives without any obstacles, it would cripple us. We would not be as strong as what we could have been. We could never fly!

51.

Life goes on –

Whether you choose to move on and take a chance in the unknown;

Or stay behind, locked in the past thinking of what could've been.

52.

WHAT IS SUCCESS?

Success is working at it.

Success is getting up and doing what you have to do every single day whether you feel like it or not.

Success is making a commitment in a particular direction and moving with fierce intensity every single day, making every single day a success in that particular direction. You don't always feel good, you don't always get what you want, but you keep going in that direction. Motivation just gets you started, it's not that hard to motivate a person, but discipline, diligence, commitment and strong habits are what gets things done…

Motivation is just a feeling; consistent action is what gets things done.

You commit once to the thing that you are going to do

and then you do it every single day.

I can't emphasize how important it is to commit to small things on a daily basis. That is what transforms you and builds you're character. When you develop your mindset along the way to your goal, not only will you have reached your goal you but you have become a different person inside.

These tiny little actions on a daily basis are what gets it done. It's not the grand vision, it's the tiny steps each day that move you toward the worthy ideal.

Being successful at something is not about feeling confident going into that situation because sometimes you don't.

It's not about knowing that it is going to work out every single time, because sometimes it doesn't... It's not about waiting until things are perfect before you started because there no such thing as perfection.

IT'S ABOUT JUST GETTING OUT THERE AND DOING IT.

Success is not about getting it right every single time because sometimes you will mess up and have to adjust what you do.

Success is about having the courage to move in the direction of your goals and dreams.

Finding out what it is that "MAKES YOUR HEART

SING" and moving in the direction that your heart is taking you every single day, that's what success is….

53.

The Importance of two simple words, "I Am."

The "I Am's" that are coming out of your mouth on a daily basis will determine your life; "I am Successful," "I am Disciplined," "I Am Amazing," "I Am full of Health," "I am Happy," "I Am Blessed," as opposed to "I am stupid," "I am a bad mother or father," "I am Fat," "I am ugly." How many times do we use the power of "I Am " against us on a daily basis? Here's the principle; Whatever follows the "I Am" will always come looking for you. I am so old; wrinkles, aches and pains come looking for you. I am fat; calories come looking for you. The good news is that you decide what you will put after the "I Am." I am Smart, I Am Strong, I am an Amazing Person. Start changing the "I Am's" and you start changing your life. What goes into your mind, comes back out in your behaviors.

(Joel Osteen)

54.

Don't worry;

Everything is going to be amazing

55.

The obstacle in our path

In ancient times, a King had a boulder placed on a roadway. Then he hid himself and watched to see if anyone would remove the huge rock. Some of the King's wealthiest merchants and courtiers came by and simply walked around it. Many loudly blamed the King for not keeping the roads clear but none did anything about getting the stone out of the way.

Then a peasant came along carrying a load of vegetables. Upon approaching the boulder, the peasant laid down his burden and tried to move the stone to the side of the road. After much pushing and straining, he finally succeeded. After the peasant picked up his load of vegetables, he noticed a purse lying in the road where the boulder had been. The purse contained many gold coins and a note from the King indicating that the gold was for the person who removed the boulder from the roadway.

The peasant learned what many of us never understand! Every obstacle presents an opportunity to improve our condition.

56.

Make this day the start of your new life. If you have been looking to change something in your life, today is that new beginning. Once you make a quality decision to change, then in that very moment, although nothing has dramatically changed, everything is different. Decide to leave that old you behind and start the process of developing a new improved version of yourself, with a definite purpose in mind.

Most people want to change but only a few are willing to go through the process of change. Changing any area of your life takes discipline, determination, patience, the ability to keep moving forward in spite of the setbacks along the way. Once you get into a mindset for change and you keep moving forward no matter what the challenges, you build your character, develop your confidence and open up the new belief that you can. Here are 3 steps to get you started:

1. Decide to take full responsibility for your life from this moment forward.
2. Once you take responsibility, you take back control of your life.
3. Start the process of renewing your mind with new information.
Take massive action on your journey to success.

57.

Why do we do the things we do? If it is so easy to change

how we think and feel then why don't we? It is easier to believe that our emotions are outside of our control. Depressed people always seems to be depressed. Happy people always seem to be happy without having to try. The truth is, we internally create our emotions by how we use our physiology, how we use our internal language and how we direct our focus. Learning how to take back control of your emotions, is the first step to taking back control of your life.

58.

The most important choice you make

Is what you choose to make important.

59.

Autobiography in Five Short Chapters

Chapter 1

I walk down the street. There is a deep hole in the sidewalk. I fall in. I am lost. I am helpless. It isn't my fault. It takes forever to find my way out.

Chapter 2

I walk down the same street. There is a deep hole in the sidewalk. I pretend I don't see it. I fall in again. I can't believe I am in the same place but it isn't my fault. It still takes me a long time to get out.

Chapter 3

I walk down the same street. There is a deep hole in the sidewalk. I see it is still there. I still fall in- it's a habit. My eyes are open. I know where I am. It is my fault. I get out immediately.

Chapter 4

I walk down the same street. There is a deep hole in the sidewalk. I walk around it.

Chapter 5

I walk down another street

(Portia Nelson)

60.

People are living their lives struggling, doing the things they don't want to do because it's easier. They are not willing to get rid of their excuses to why they can't achieve their goals. We seem to live in a microwave world where we want things to happen instantly or we give up. There are going to be tests that you need to pass in life; negative thinking, bad days, negative people etc. When you want more out of life, you have to start having some consistency. Success is an all-time thing, it's not a once in a while thing.

61.

A question works because unlike a statement, which requires you to obey, a question requires you to think. The mind seems to prefer to think, not to obey.

(Nancy Kine)

62.

When people come to see me and I ask them what they really want, most of the time the answer is the same, "I don't really know." If you don't know what you want you continue to drift, feeling unfulfilled, frustrated with life and unhappy. Everything starts with your vision. You can have the greatest ship in the world, but if the captain doesn't know where he's going, it means nothing. What do you really want for your life? What is going to give you fulfilment? Not success on somebody else's terms. Success without fulfilment is ultimate failure. Decide what you want and turn it into a must. Ask yourself the question, "What do I really want for my life?" Reignite that passion and then ask yourself, " What would I do if I knew I couldn't fail?" By simply asking yourself new questions, you send your subconscious mind in a new direction. Remember it's your mind, it's there to give you what you want, you just have to set the direction.

63.

Changing any area of your life is simply about developing new habits in a certain direction. Then having the discipline and doing the daily things that will move you in the direction you want to go. Building a new habit is like a rocket ship that is launched into space; It needs all that thrust to lift it off the ground. Those boosters are shooting it up into the air but in a little while, once it gets into outer space, it doesn't need all that extra energy, it simply had to press past the earth's atmosphere. In the same way we are developing new habits. At first it seems difficult but if you will stick with it, you'll come to a point where it's not difficult at all, it will become natural to you. Being consistent is the key. It's better to suffer a little while than to suffer the pain of defeat for the rest of your life and look back with regret and think, "I should have" or "if I had just made the effort." A lot of people go to their graves with their natural talent not expressed due to laziness or fear or excuses. Don't let that be you. If you have a talent inside of you, start small and get into the habit of getting that talent out into the world. We only get one chance at life, we can't go back and give it another shot. So why let your excuses stop you from being the person you really want to be? You don't need to take on the world all at once. One small step at a time gets you started and you gain your confidence along the way.

64.

Just because something isn't happening in your life right now;

Doesn't mean that it will never happen.

Developing the skill of patience is an important ingredient in continued success.

(Robert Herdman)

65.

Don't Give It Up

Today life gave you another slap
but don't give it up,
throwing your towel in the ring
for things gone wrong, for words that sting,
'cos there must be another way,
you will see it in the light of another day.

When everything seems sour, not in your favour,
look around until you find better flavor.
So, don't just give up, but live it up.
pick up the pieces, be tough,

> grind your teeth and turn another cheek.
> Don't give it up, that's exactly what they seek,
> It's too easy to walk away.
>
> A quitter never wins so you should better stay,
> look challenges straight in the eye.
> Don't say yet the last good-bye,
> fight like an animal in a trap
> but don't give it up.
>
> (Z. Vujcic)

66.

In your quiet moments, what do you think about? How far you've come or how far you have to go? Your strengths or your weaknesses? The best that might happen or the worst that could happen? In your quiet moments, pay attention to your thoughts. Because maybe, just maybe, the only thing that needs to shift in order for you to experience more happiness, more love, and more vitality, is your way of thinking. Everything you do on the outside world is a result of how your thinking has been. Remember thoughts are just that: thoughts. They have no power until you emotionally charge them. But it's never the first thought or the second thought that causes you to feel down, depressed, stress or anxious, it's the tenth, the hundredth, the ones you focus on all day long. Remember when a negative thought comes to mind, say to yourself, "that's simply just a thought, it doesn't mean anything" and decide to move on focusing on something that will be more beneficial to your day. The pattern for changing anything in your life starts with changing how you think.

67.

It doesn't matter what happens to you;

What matters is what you are going to do about it.

68.

You either pay the price of success or the price of regret.

The price of success weighs ounces.

The price of regret weighs tons.

It's Your Choice.

(Ruben Gonzalex, Three-time Olympian)

69.

Are you in control of your emotions or are your emotions in control of you? Every emotion you experience is a direct response to a thought, not to the world around you. The clearer you see that your emotions are reactions to your thoughts, not to the world, the easier it is to simply feel them and let them go. The gift of that insight, is that you stop needing to change the world in order to change how you feel from moment to moment. You are in control of how you feel, not your circumstances or the people around you.

70.

The Woodcutter

Once upon a time there was a very strong wood-cutter. He asked for a job from a timber merchant and he got it. The pay was very good and so were the work conditions so for that reason, the wood-cutter was determined to do his very best. His boss gave him an axe and showed him the area in the forest where he was to work. The first day the wood-cutter cut down eighteen trees. His boss was extremely impressed and said, "Well done. Keep it up. You are our best wood-cutter yet." Motivated by his boss's words, the wood-cutter tried even harder the next day but he only cut down fifteen trees. The third day he tried even harder but only cut down ten trees, even though he was working just as hard as he did on day one. Day after day the woodcutter cut down fewer and fewer trees. Knowing his potential and seeing how hard the man was working everyday, the boss came to him and told him that he needed to be more productive to keep his job. The wood-cutter needed the job, so he tried harder and harder. He started working extra hours, during his lunch breaks and tea breaks, but he still could not cut down enough trees. "I must be losing my strength," the wood-cutter thought to himself. He worked over-time but still it was not enough. Eventually his boss came to him and told him he was fired. The wood-cutter was really upset but he knew that he had worked as hard as he could and just did not have enough time to chop more trees. He sadly handed his axe back.

The boss took one look at the axe and asked, "When was the last time you sharpened this axe?"

"Sharpen my axe?" the wood-cutter replied. "I have never sharpened my axe. I have been too busy trying to cut down enough trees." Moral of the story: Don't get too busy that you don't take time to sharpen your axe.

(Stephen Covey)

Renewing your mind on a daily basis is a simple way of sharpening your axe each day. When you take the time out of your day to put good stuff into your mind and condition those new thoughts and ideas through repetition, you live each day with a healthier mindset.

When your mind is healthy; stress, depression and anxiety

cannot stay in your life.

Renewing your mind is not a onetime event, it is an ongoing endeavor, it has to become a habit.

71.

Things only happen to you in life when you make a commitment to changing yourself from the inside out. When you keep putting things off, you're committing to staying the same. If you're unhappy with any area in your life, it's up to you to take back control. We all have the power inside to change in an instant and that first step is simply to make a decision that you will change now. Don't worry about how this will happen. Once you make the commitment, things start to happen.

72.

Success is a process, not a single event.

There is a process to follow in everything we do in life and when you follow the process, things start to happen. If you don't follow the process, you don't get the results, it's that simple.

Take successful people in any profession for instance. The lawyer studies and practices law on a daily basis to be successful in his profession, he follows a process. The doctor studies and practices medicine on a daily basis to become successful at what she does, she follows a process. An athlete first studies and then practices their craft on a daily basis to become a champion, they follow a process. But when most people want to change any area of their lives, they try something once or twice and if that doesn't work, they move onto something else and then something else. It's never their fault, so they blame other things, other people or they develop their story and that story becomes their platform, which they regurgitate consistently to justify why they have not succeeded. A lot of people are not successful in life, not because they don't have the ability or talent to be successful, but because they are just too bloody lazy to become successful. They want for change to happen in their lives right now, with as little effort as possible on their part. They want to get a hundred percent out and are only willing to put in one or two percent (if even that) and they want to do that over and over again, constantly moving from one thing to the next with no commitment on their part. They want what I call, "the magic wand treatment," their attitude being, wave your magic wand and fix me; make me successful, make me slimmer, take away my depression, make me financially independent but make sure there's no effort on my part.

Being successful at anything in life is not an easy process but it is a very simple process, that when you follow a structure you can enjoy the fruits of success. If you are not willing to get actively involved and follow the process, then success will elude you. You are in control of what happens, no one else.

73.

Don't Quit

When things go wrong, as they sometimes will,

When the road you're trudging seems all uphill,

When the funds are low and the debts are high,

And you want to smile, but you have to sigh,

When care is pressing you down a bit-

Rest if you must, but don't you quit.

Life is queer with its twists and turns,

As every one of us sometimes learns,

And many a fellow turns about

When he might have won had he stuck it out.

Don't give up though the pace seems slow -

You may succeed with another blow.

Often the goal is nearer than

It seems to a faint and faltering man;

Often the struggler has given up
When he might have captured the victor's cup;
And he learned too late when the night came down,
How close he was to the golden crown.
Success is failure turned inside out -
The silver tint in the clouds of doubt,
And you never can tell how close you are,
It might be near when it seems afar;
So stick to the fight when you're hardest hit -
It's when things seem worst that you must not quit.

(unknown)

74.

What is necessary to change a person-

Is to change his awareness of himself.

(A.Maslow)

75.

So much doom and gloom around us at the moment, if you focus on it, it is easy to get caught up. What you continuously focus on in life, you manifest. If you are reading this stop for a moment and ask yourself these questions, "What am I grateful for in my life right now?"...."Who or what makes me happy at this moment in time?"...."Who do I love and who loves me?"

Changing your focus can ultimately change your life, no matter how hard things seem in the moment. Nothing in life has any meaning, only the meaning you decide to give to it. Learn to enjoy every minute of your life. Be happy right now. Don't wait for something outside of yourself to make you happy in the future.

Every minute you have should be enjoyed and savored. We create our destiny everyday we live. Life doesn't have to be perfect, it just has to be lived.

76.

It's time to take your life back from the people that are causing you pain and making you unhappy.

This is your life and you are the author of your story.

If you're stuck on the same page, just remember that at any moment, you have the power to write a new chapter.

77.

The world we are experiencing today is a result of our

creative consciousness,

And if we want a new world, each of us must start taking responsibility for helping create it.

(Rosemary Fillmore Rhea)

78.

If you're focused on the negative, there could be all sorts of positive things and opportunities happening right before your very eyes and you don't even notice. If you focus on the problem, there could be a solution right in front of you and you walk right pass it. As obvious as that solution may be, if you get too focused in the wrong direction, it can actually blind you to certain realities. Start focusing on where you want to go in life, not where you've been. You can't change the past but there is an amazing future out there waiting for you.

79.

The only person you are destined to become,

is the person you decide to be.

(Ralph Waldo Emmerson)

80.

Knowledge is only potential power.

Taking that knowledge and coming up with an action plan that you work everyday is what changes your world.

81.

Our expectations set the limits for our life. Most people go through life not expecting the right things. They don't expect to get anywhere in life. They don't expect the good breaks. They don't realise their own wrong thinking is keeping them from achieving what they want. Life meets us at the level of our expectations. If we expect a little, we receive a little. If we don't expect anything to get better, it probably won't. You need to pay attention to what you are expecting. If you start raising your levels of expectancy and start expecting more from life, then the law of attraction reciprocates what we put out there. For everyone that is reading this message when was the last time you got out of bed and started off your day by saying, "something amazing is going to happen to me today." We have to set the tone for the day right at the very beginning. Your expectation is your faith at work. Have faith in yourself that you are better than what you are putting out there and expect for things to happen.

Remember your expectations are setting the limits for your life. You've got to expect for things to happen and have faith on the inside before it will ever happen on the outside.

82.

Yesterday, Today and Tomorrow

There are two days in every week that we should not worry about, two days that should be kept free from fear and apprehension.

One is yesterday, with its mistakes and cares, its faults and blunders, its aches and pains. Yesterday has passed, forever beyond our control.

All the money in the world cannot bring back yesterday. We cannot undo a single act we performed. Nor can we erase a single word we've said - yesterday is gone!

The other day we shouldn't worry about is tomorrow, with its impossible adversaries, its burden, its hopeful promise and poor performance. Tomorrow is beyond our control.

Tomorrow's sun will rise either in splendour or behind a mask of clouds - but it will rise. And until it does, we have no stake in tomorrow, for it is yet unborn.

This leaves only one day - today. Any person can fight the battles of just one day. It is only when we add the burdens of yesterday and tomorrow that we break down.

It is not the experience of today that drives people mad - it is the remorse of bitterness for something which happened yesterday, and the dread of what tomorrow may bring.

Let us, therefore, live one day at a time!

(unknown)

83.

When you are faced with a situation in life, become solution orientated instead of problem oriented. If you're in a situation that you have no control over, then there's no point worrying about it because you have no control over it. Alternatively, if there is something you can do in that moment to take back control, then go do what you need to do to take back control. When you are faced with a situation that you would normally worry about, instead of letting worry dominate your mind, ask yourself these simple questions;

What else could this mean to me?

If I wasn't spending my energy right now worrying about this situation, what could I be doing instead, to solve this problem and get a different result that would benefit me and all involved?

Write down a list of a few possible alternatives you could do that would get you a new result.

When you start asking yourself better questions, you will be amazed how you're mind will search for better results. When people are limited in their thinking, they are limited in their lives.

A simple shift in your thinking and asking yourself a better set of questions, can totally change the outcome. Human beings are capable of the most amazing things when they decide to stop worrying and make a new decision to take back control of their lives.

84.

The mistake people make is that they try to control the thoughts that come into their head on a daily basis. We cannot control the many thoughts that pass through our minds. It's not the thoughts that pass through your head that impact your life, it's the ones you take ownership of and think about all day long. It's almost never the first thought that hurts- it's when you allow your mind to follow a negative train of thoughts on a journey to a destination you don't want to be. You always have a choice and if you're in a negative mindset right now, you have simply chosen to focus on and give your energy to the wrong train of thoughts. If what you're doing right now is not working for you, now is the time to change the thoughts you focus on and start to direct your focus and energy to a different train of thoughts. What about starting with this; take a moment and think to yourself, "what and who am I grateful for in my life right now?" "Who do I love and what is it about them that I love?"

85.

A Superior Attitude

The more I live, the more I realise the impact of attitude on life.

Attitude to me is more important than facts.

It is more important than the past, than education, than money, than circumstances, than failures, than successes, than what other people think, say or do.

It is more important than appearance, giftedness, or skill.

It will make or break a company, a school, a home.

The remarkable thing is, that we have a choice everyday regarding the attitude we will embrace for that day.

We cannot change the past.

We cannot change the fact that people will act in a certain way.

We cannot change the inevitable.

The only thing we can do is plan on the one thing we have and that is our superior attitude.

I am convinced that life is 10% what happens to me,

and 90% how I react to it.

A superior attitude will produce superior results.

86.

Take the next couple of days off from your problems.

They will still be there when you get back, but with a few days off you could see them from a totally different perspective.

87.

We have the illusion that being happy and having a sense of wellbeing seems to be marked by having the right stuff;

money, relationship, nice home, job etc. Wellbeing is not the fruit of something you do or have. It is the essence of who you are. There is nothing you need to change, do, be or have in order to be happy. When you begin to understand that wellbeing and happiness is your nature, not a goal to be pursued, you will realise that all you need to do to get it back, is to turn your attention from the outside inwards. Happiness and wellbeing is simply a choice. Choose to be happy now for who you are and what you have in this moment.

88.

God's delays are not God's denials. A little bit of patience, persistence and a little faith will eventually get you there. No matter what the obstacles, keep in mind just because you don't know the answer doesn't mean that one does not exist. You simply haven't discovered it yet.

89.

Forget all the reasons why it won't work and believe the one reason why it will.

(Unknown)

90.

Building Bridges

Once upon a time two brothers who lived on adjoining farms fell into conflict. It was the first serious rift in 40 years of farming side by side, sharing machinery and trading labour and goods as needed without a hitch.

Then the long collaboration fell apart. It began with a small misunderstanding and it grew into a major difference. Finally it exploded into an exchange of bitter words followed by weeks of silence.

One morning there was a knock on John's door. He opened it to find a man with a carpenter's toolbox. "I'm looking for a few days work," he said.

"Perhaps you would have a few small jobs here and there. Could I help you?"

"Yes," said the older brother. "I do have a job for you. Look across the creek at that farm. That's my neighbour, in fact, it's my younger brother. Last week there was a meadow between us and he took his bulldozer to the river levee and now there is a creek between us. Well, he may have done this to spite me, but I'll go him one better. See that pile of lumber curing by the barn? I want you to build me a fence - an 8-foot fence - so I won't need to see his place anymore. Cool him down, anyhow."

The carpenter said, "I think I understand the situation.

Show me the nails and the post-hole digger and I'll be able to do a job that pleases you."

The older brother had to go to town for supplies, so he helped the carpenter get the materials ready and then he was off for the day.

The carpenter worked hard all that day measuring, sawing, nailing.

About sunset when the farmer returned, the carpenter had just finished his job. The farmer's eyes opened wide, his jaw dropped.

There was no fence there at all. It was a bridge, a bridge stretching from one side of the creek to the other! A fine piece of work handrails and all - and the neighbour, his younger brother, was coming across, his hand outstretched.

"You are quite a fellow to build this bridge after all I've said and done."

The two brothers stood at each end of the bridge and then they met in the middle, taking each other's hand. They turned to see the carpenter hoist his toolbox on his shoulder. "No, wait! Stay a few days. I've a lot of other projects for you," said the older brother.

"I'd love to stay on," the carpenter said, "but, I have many more bridges to build."

91.

"You have to believe that you can be whatever you want to be.

If you are willing to pay the price and to work for your goals, you will find that others are willing to work with you and for you, to help you reach your potential. Enthusiasm and work ethic are contagious. Is yours worth catching?"

92.

The best way to move forward in life

is to let go of the things that are holding you back.

93.

What do you see when you look in the mirror? How many people reading this honestly look in the mirror and really love what they see? When I say love, I don't mean a cocky, conceited feeling, I mean an honest true contentment of yourself. Someone you love being around. Your sub-conscious self-image is how you think you look in spite of what everyone else thinks of you. If you don't love what you see looking back from the mirror, how can you expect others to have that opinion of you? Genuine confidence, contentment and happiness, is loving what you see looking back at you in that mirror.

94.

This is your world. Shape it or someone else will.

95.

To change your life, you need to think big and act small. Work on the only thing that you have direct control over, which is yourself, your attitudes and your actions. Everything begins with you. Remember that these seven small words make up the strongest sentence in the English language.

"IF IT IS TO BE, IT IS UP TO ME."

96.

You can't change your life when you have an old traditional way of thinking.

Maybe you're going through some things in your life that you're struggling with and you don't know how to break those bonds and move forward.

The first key to transformation is that you've got to take your mind off yourself. You've got to take your mind off your problems and your circumstances. You have got to start focusing your mind on solutions and taking small steps to turn things around in your life.

Because whether you want to hear it or not, no matter what you are going through in your life right now, no matter how bad things may seem, you are the only one in your life that can turn it around. Other people can guide you and help you through change but you have to take responsibility for your own life and make the decision that you are the only one that can turn things around. You have to be aware how a mental diet is the key to transforming your life.

When you want to lose weight you need to watch what you eat. Stop doing the things that lead you to become over weight; over eating, snacking in between meals. All these things are basis principles of weight loss and if you apply consistently on a daily basis, they work If you want to change any area of your life you have to make the necessary time to do the things that need to be done for that change to take place in your life. If you don't have the time to implement those changes, then things are not going to change for you and it's that simple.

Changing anything in your life is about developing new habits. It's about turning up each day and putting in the effort, consistence, persistence, diligence and moving forward.

97.

Excuses are excuses,

no matter what way you look at it.

98.

The Victor

If you think you are beaten, you are.
If you think you dare not, you don't.
If you like to win but think you can't,
It's almost a cinch you won't.
If you think you'll lose, you're lost.
For out in the world we find
Success begins with a fellow's will.
It's all in the state of mind.
If you think you are out classed, you are.
You've got to think high to rise.
You've got to be sure of your-self before
You can ever win the prize.
Life's battles don't always go
To the stronger or faster man.
But sooner or later, the man who wins
Is the man who thinks he can.

(C.W. Longenecker)

99.

As human beings we are driven by our emotions. People don't necessarily remember what you said to them, they remember how you made them feel. So think of the people you were talking to yesterday. Imagine how your words made them feel. If you know that what you said made them feel sad, hurt, angry or negative in any way, then how could you go about today by changing it and saying something that will make them feel wonderful?

100.

You are what you do,

not what you say you'll do.

(C. G. Jung)

101.

We don't get what we want in life, we get what we expect. If you expect to be successful then eventually that's what will happen, but if you expect for things to go wrong then eventually they will. What the mind expects tends to be realised. Start expecting for things to go your way and through practice, the law of attraction will start working for you.

102.

Remember this; with every experience in which you look fear in the face,

You gain inner strength and confidence.

So spread your wings, open doors and go for it.

(Lisa Desatnik)

103.

Happiness is not a result, it's a state of mind. Most people are about as happy as they make up their minds to be. The important thing to remember is that happiness is first and foremost a choice. Decide to go out into the world today and choose to be happy no matter what challenges you face. When you choose your emotions, you bring that energy into your day. You don't have to believe it, just try it and see what happens.

104.

Any day you wish, you can discipline yourself to change anything in your life. Any day you wish, you can open your mind to new knowledge. Any day you wish, you can start a new activity. Any day you wish, you can start the process of changing your life. You can do it today or next week or next year. You can also do nothing. You can pretend rather than perform. And if the idea of having to change yourself makes you uncomfortable, you can remain just as you are. You can choose rest over labour, entertainment over education, delusion over truth and doubt over confidence. The choices are yours to make. If you are happy with your life then you have an amazing gift but if you don't like how things are, then change it. You have the ability to totally transform any area in your life and it begins with your very own power of choice. You alone created your current circumstances by the past choices you made. You alone have the ability and responsibility to make better choices beginning today. You create your own world. The power to change your world is within your hands.

105.

You are what you are and where you are because of what has gone into your mind. You can change what you are and where you are, by changing what goes into your mind. Don't let negative people and criticism affect your judgement about yourself. Remember, the only taste of success some people have, is when they take a bite out of you. Have the confidence in yourself to rise above the nay sayers of this world. Walk through life making your own decisions with your head held high.

106.

For to be free is not merely to cast off one's chains, but to live in a way that respects and enhances the freedom of others.

(Nelson Mandela)

107.

Your own motivation in life is what keeps you going and excites you to live. Having a dream and a true passion to do what you love is what living is all about. Take the extra step and do whatever is necessary to make yourself unique. Be the absolute best at what you take pleasure in and let nothing stop you from reaching your aspirations. Do not allow yourself to get hung up on things that have already happened or worry about things that may happen. Concentrate on what you are shooting for right now and everything else will take care of itself. The problem with most people is that they don't know what they want. If you don't know what you want how can you achieve it? Once you know exactly what you want to achieve in life, you set the wheels in motions.

108.

When you want to change any area of your life you SET

your mind by making a quality decision of what it is you really want, (not what you think you should have). You don't set your mind according to your circumstances.

You don't set your mind according to other people's opinions of how successful they think you will be. You don't set your mind according to fear or failure. You set your mind on what you want and what it is going to take to get you there.

Your first focus is making the decision and making the commitment that you are going to follow through. So much of our lives is on automatic pilot that we sometimes don't see how we can change.

Any breakthrough you're going to have in your life starts with making that quality decision and then going through a process of changing those old beliefs by renewing your mind on a daily basis.

No matter what you are trying to achieve; a better relationship, building a new business, becoming financially independent or whatever success means to you, it is so important to develop the mindset of the person you want to become along the way. This is how the changes last and the success continues. If your mindset stays the same, then your life stays the same.

If your mindset stays the same, then your marriage or your relationship stays the same.

If your mindset stays the same, then your business stays the same.

The truth is that nothing ever stays the same; we are either growing or we are dying.

For true change to happen and continue in any area of your life, you have got to change the way you think along the way to your goal or dream.

109.

A lot of people have been conditioned to confuse their "Identity" with their behaviours. People say to me all the time, "oh that's just the way I am and there's nothing I can do about it." My response is, "that's not the way you are and there's everything you can do about it." The truth is that some people are just too lazy to be successful. You have got to do your part and take responsibility for your actions. Life is not a quick fix, sometimes it takes a bit of effort to move out of pain into pleasure. It's up to you to take control of your life.

110.

"I wasn't satisfied just to earn a good living. I was looking to make a statement."
(Donald Trump)

111.

Never let life's gossips or nay Sayers disturb you. A person's mind that worries or gets involved in what people are saying or thinking about them, soon gets caught up in that very action. Remember what we constantly think about, is what we manifest in our lives. Let others gossip while you choose your future and work hard to achieve it. When you eventually achieve your goal, the gossip will still be doing what they're good at. As we get older, it's the person that we become inside that matters.

112.

Live life on your terms and not someone else's. Stand up for what you believe, not what someone else wants you to believe. Take charge of your own destiny, don't let others dictate your future. Don't live your life trying to be like someone else, be yourself. Everyone else is already taken.

113.

All things splendid have been achieved by those who dared believe that something inside them was superior to circumstances.

114.

I truly believe that to be at the pinnacle of any game or whatever you do in life,

You have got to be a little bit gone,

You have got to be almost insane to your craft,

Seeing it in your mind long before it happens and not a lot of people can understand that.

(Connor McGregor, World Champion MMA Fighter)

115.

It is your world;

shape it or someone else will.

116.

One of the biggest mistakes people make in life is that they don't take any time out of their day to relax and unwind. The world we live in is becoming so fast and people are becoming easier stressed. Getting into the habit of taking 20/30 minutes to switch off and just relax each day is one of the most important things you can do for your mental and physical wellbeing. Get into the habit of doing nothing for 30 minutes. It's easier than you think; no complicated techniques, nothing to focus on, no television, no computer, no phone, just close your eyes, take a few deep breaths and let your consciousness detach and drift, while your subconscious mind enjoys the physical and emotional benefits of the relaxation experience. You'll be surprised how great you feel after. Go ahead give it a go.

117.

Life meets us at the level of our expectations. If we expect a little from life, we receive a little. If we don't expect for anything to get better, it probably won't. If we started to train ourselves to raise our level of expectancy and started expecting more from life, the law of attraction would reciprocate what we put out there. What if everyone reading this post got out of bed tomorrow and said, "something amazing is going to happen to me today," and truly expected that to happen, how would things turn out? I suppose there's only one way to find out.

118.

If Not Now, when?

119.

Potatoes, Eggs, and Coffee Beans

Once upon a time a daughter complained to her father that her life was miserable and that she didn't know how she was going to make it. She was tired of fighting and struggling all the time. It seemed just as one problem was solved, another one soon followed.

Her father, a chef, took her to the kitchen. He filled three pots with water and placed each on a high fire. Once the three pots began to boil, he placed potatoes in one pot, eggs in the second pot and ground coffee beans in the third pot.

He then let them sit and boil without saying a word to his daughter. The daughter moaned and impatiently waited, wondering what he was doing.

After twenty minutes he turned off the burners. He took the potatoes out of the pot and placed them in a bowl. He pulled the eggs out and placed them in a bowl.

He then ladled the coffee out and placed it in a cup. Turning to her he asked. "Daughter, what do you see?"

"Potatoes, eggs, and coffee," she hastily replied.

"Look closer," he said, "and touch the potatoes." She did and noted that they were soft. He then asked her to take an egg and break it. After pulling off the shell, she observed the hard-boiled egg. Finally, he asked her to sip the coffee. It's rich aroma brought a smile to her face.

"Father, what does this mean?" she asked.

He then explained that the potatoes, the eggs and coffee beans had each faced the same adversity– the boiling water.

However, each one reacted differently.

The potato went in strong, hard, and unrelenting, but in boiling water, it became soft and weak.

The egg was fragile, with the thin outer shell protecting its liquid interior until it was put in the boiling water. Then the inside of the egg became hard.

However, the ground coffee beans were unique. After they were exposed to the boiling water, they changed the water and created something new.

"Which are you," he asked his daughter. "When adversity knocks on your door, how do you respond? Are you a potato, an egg, or a coffee bean?"

Moral: In life, things happen around us, things happen to us, but the only thing that truly matters is what happens within us.

Which one are you?

120.

Imagine if you had the ability to achieve anything you wanted in your life? The truth is you do. What the mind expects to happen usually does. The question is this, years from now, will you look back on life and say, "I wish I had," or "I'm glad I did?

121.

What is the meaning of your life?

Whatever you want it to be.

(James Frey)

122.

Enter a room or a meeting like you own the place

123.

Progress is impossible without change,

And those who cannot change their minds cannot change anything.

(George Bernard Shaw)

124.

We don't get what we want in life, we get what we expect. If you expect to be successful then that's what happens but if you expect for things to go wrong then eventually they will. WHAT THE MIND EXPECTS TENDS TO BE REALISED. Start living your life expecting things to happen and you'll soon reap what you sow.

125.

A: Action

C: Changes

T: Things

126.

Success

To laugh often and much,
To win the respect of intelligent people and the affection of children,
To earn the appreciation of honest critics and endure the betrayal of false friends,
To appreciate beauty,
To find the best in others,
To leave the world a bit better, whether by a healthy

child,
A garden patch or a redeemed social condition,
To know even one life has breathed easier because you have lived.
This is to have succeeded.

(Ralph Waldo Emmerson)

127.

When you overcome a challenging period in your life, you're better off when you get up from that challenge because you have experienced a taste of failure and moved beyond it. In life there is no such thing as failure, just results that you can learn from. The only failure is if you give up on life completely. I have recently just worked with a lady who's life had fell apart 10 years ago and over the last 2 weeks she has experienced what it is to live and love life again. Remember, there's always a way if you're committed.

128.

When you're in one of those situations or times in your life, when everything goes against you, till it seems as though you could not hold on a minute longer, never give up, for that is just the place and time when the tide will turn. At these points in our lives we must suffer one of two things; the pain of discipline or the pain of regret or disappointment. Winston Churchill summed it up in seven simple words, "When you're going through hell, keep going".

129.

We sometimes get caught up with the problems we are faced with in life...Problems are an inevitable part of life.....When you are faced with a problem, think of it as a challenge; hold your head up high and think I am bigger than you, you cannot defeat me. If you think you can overcome any challenge that comes into your life, you will. You control the most important tool in success, your mind. You have your own world in your own hands to control...No one else but you decides were you go in life.

130.

Cowards die many times before their deaths; the valiant never taste of death but once.

(William Shakespeare)

131.

Do not look back and grieve over the past,

for it's gone;

Do not be troubled about the future

For it has not come yet;

Live in the present, and make it so beautiful

That it will be worth remembering.

132.

Don't let the weeds grow around your dreams. Judge your success by what you had to give up to get what you want. Along the way to your success take good care of your reputation and your attitude, they are the most valuable assets you have. Remember you can miss a lot of good things in life by having the wrong attitude so take care of it. Don't let someone else choose it for you. Your life, your attitude: your success.

133.

Motivation is that mental bridge between a thought and an action. I believe if you want to stay motivated on a daily basis, it's a bit like exercise. If you want to become fit for instance, you don't just go down to the gym one time and, and that's the job done. If you don't exercise on a regular basis, then you rapidly lose whatever benefits you get from it. To keep yourself motivated, you need to be doing something on a regular basis. You need to be programming yourself on a regular basis to make your motivated state a habit, that you can access when you need it. If you don't take the time out of your day to recondition your brain for success, then you're merely running at a fraction of your potential.

134.

"I bargained with Life for a penny,
And Life would pay no more,
However I begged at evening
When I counted my scanty store;

For Life is just an employer,
He gives you what you ask,
But once you have set the wages,
Why, you must bear the task.

I worked for a menial's hire,
Only to learn, dismayed,
That any wage I had asked of Life,
Life would have paid."

(Jessie B. Rittenhouse)

135.

You lose energy when life becomes dull in your mind. Your mind gets bored and therefore tired of doing nothing. The more you lose yourself in something bigger, the more energy you will have. You don't have time to think about yourself and get bogged down in your emotional difficulties. To live with constant energy it is important to get your emotional state in check. Negative emotions drain energy. You will never have full energy until you get your emotional faults corrected. People who lack energy are disorganised to one degree or another by their deep, fundamental, emotional and psychological conflicts.

136.

Life is not about finding yourself;

It's about creating yourself.

137.

When you're stuck in a situation and can't seem to move forward, it's not that you're doing the wrong thing...It's just that you're not doing the right thing long enough. Consistency is the key to any breakthrough in life. You have got to take the time daily to digest what it is you want instead; into your sub-conscious mind and let that knowledge unfold. It's your mind, it's there to give you what you want. You just have to condition it daily.

138.

A Boy with a Dream

Let me share with you a short story;

It's a story about a young boy who was the son of a travelling horse trainer who would go from town to town, stable to stable, race track to race track, farm to farm and ranch to ranch, training horses.

As a result, the boy's high school career was continually interrupted because he had to travel a lot with his father and missed a lot of school.

When he was a senior, he was asked to write a paper about what he wanted to be and do when he grew up.

That night he wrote a seven-page paper describing his goal of someday owning a horse ranch.

He wrote about his dream in great detail and he even drew a diagram of a 200-acre ranch, showing the location of all the buildings, the stables and the track.

Then he drew a detailed floor plan for a 4,000-square-foot house that would sit on a 200-acre dream ranch.

He put a great deal of his heart into the project and the next day he handed it in to his teacher.

Two days later he received his paper back.

On the front page was a large red F with a note that read, "See me after class,"

The boy with the dream went to see the teacher after class and asked,

"Why did I receive an F?"

The teacher said,

"This is an unrealistic dream for a young boy like you, you have no money, you come from an average family, you have no resources.

Owning a horse ranch requires a lot of money.

You have to buy the land, you have to pay for the original breeding stock and later you'll have to pay large stud fees, there's no way you could ever do it."

Then the teacher added, `If you will rewrite this paper with a more realistic goal, I will reconsider your grade.'

"The boy went home and thought about it long and hard

He asked his father what he should do.

His father said, `Look, son, you have to make up your own mind on this.

However, I think it is a very important decision for you.'

"Finally, after sitting with it for a week, the boy turned in the same paper, making no changes at all, except for one.

On the front page in large red writing he wrote,

"You can keep your F and I'll keep my dream."

He was brought to the head master and given detention for 3 days for his remarks.

Fifteen years later that same boy became one of the top horse breeders in his state in America.

His name is Monty Roberts and he lives in a 4,000-square-foot house in the middle of a 200-acre horse ranch.

He still has that school paper which he has framed over the fireplace.

The best part of the story is that two summers ago that same schoolteacher brought 30 kids to camp out on my ranch for a week.

When he came to the ranch he introduced himself to Monty as his teacher and Monty brought him into his living room and showed him the framed test paper above his fireplace.

When the teacher was leaving, he said, "Look, Monty, I can tell you this now, when I was your teacher, I was something of a dream stealer.

During those years I stole a lot of kids' dreams.

Fortunately you had enough gumption not to give up on yours."

Moral of the story is this:

No 1: Don't let anyone steal your dreams. Follow your heart, no matter what.

No 2…You need to decide what it is you want and then have a game plan.

Get a structure and put it into place and follow that plan diligently every day.

No dream is too big or too small when you work hard to live it.

139.

The best thing about the past is that it's over. When people don't deal with the past as if it's over, then they're not free to go into the future. The only way your past affects you is if you're living there every day. As human beings we tend to feel bad almost habitually because of our past. Whatever you have done in the past is not a reflection of your possibilities it's just a reflection of your consciousness. No one knows what you are capable of and where you can go in life. You don't even know that.

By focusing on what you want in the future and visualizing this in your mind over and over, you are giving your sub-conscious a new direction. Remember the past does not equal the future, only if you live there constantly. All of us have within us the power to change our personal history. Changing our thinking of who we are and what is possible for us...

LET THE PAST GO, SO THAT YOU CAN GROW.

140.

Your own motivation in life is what keeps you going and excites you to live. Having a dream and a true passion to do what you love is what living is all about. Take that extra step and do whatever is necessary to make yourself unique. Be the absolute best at what you take pleasure in and let nothing stop you from reaching your aspirations. Do not allow yourself to get hung up on things that have already happened or worry about things that may happen. Concentrate and focus on what you're shooting for right now and everything else will take care of itself.

141.

Wine is constant proof that God loves us and loves to see us happy.

(Benjamin Franklin)

142.

Whenever I have faced a setback I have dusted myself down and got on with the rest of my life because I believed in myself.

(Sir Philip Green)

143.

Sometimes the people around you won't understand your journey.

They don't need to-

It's not for them.

144.

Once a person's mind is expanded with an idea or concept it can never be satisfied to going back to where it was. Visualize the dream that you have for your life, see it in your mind every day with the intention of achieving it and your mind will bring you closer to achieving it, no matter what it may be. Napoleon Hill once said,

"What the mind can conceive and believe, the mind will achieve."

145.

Our attitudes control our lives. Attitudes are a secret power working 24 hours a day, for good or bad. It is of paramount importance that we know how to harness and control this great force. It's not what happens to us in life but the attitude we take into and out of those situations that matter. Your attitude is the greatest tool you can have. Start by living in an attitude of gratitude. Be grateful for what you have in life, others are not so fortunate.

146.

As human beings we do not act directly on the world around us. Each of us creates a representation of the world in which we live. Our representation of the world then determines, to a large degree, what our experience of the world will be; how we perceive the world and what choices we will see available to us. For anyone to change a behavior that is creating a negative effect in their lives, e.g. depression, fears, phobias, etc. we have to change how we represent this in our minds. All negative behavior is just that, a behavior, that can easily be changed...Change happens the moment you represent the same event in your mind in a different, more empowering way. No Exceptions.

147.

The Road Not Taken

Two roads diverged in a yellow wood,
And sorry I could not travel both
And be one traveler, long I stood
And looked down one as far as I could
To where it bent in the undergrowth;
Then took the other, just as fair,
And having perhaps the better claim,
Because it was grassy and wanted wear;
Though as for that passing there
Had worn them really about the same,
And both that morning equally lay
In leaves no step had trodden black.
Oh, I kept the first for another day!
Yet knowing how way leads to way,
I doubted if I should ever come back.
Somewhere ages and ages hence:
Two roads diverged in a wood, and I -
I took the one less traveled by,
And that has made all the difference.

(Robert Frost)

148.

Wealth is the product of man's ability to think

(Ayn Rand)

149.

The simple formula for changing any area of your life: one day at a time. Be the best you can be today and see how many good today's you can put together. Simply focus on that and you have built a new habit.

150.

I like long walks, especially when they are taken by people who annoy me.

(Fred Allen)

151.

You Can Be Whatever You Want to Be

There is inside you
All of the potential
To be whatever you want to be;
All of the energy
To do whatever you want to do.

Imagine yourself as you would like to be,
Doing what you want to do,
And each day, take one step
Towards your dream.
And though at times it may seem too
difficult to continue,
Hold on to your dream.
One morning you will awake to find
That you are the person you dreamed of,
Doing what you wanted to do,
Simply because you had the courage
To believe in your potential
And to hold on to your dream.

You Can Do it! We Can Do It.

(Donna Levine)

152.

The Abbot and the Monk

Many thousands of years ago, or so the story goes, the word of God was transcribed into written form. Because there were no word processors, photocopiers or even printing presses, monks would painstakingly copy each original text by hand. It could easily take a year to complete even one document.

A young monk who had abandoned the search for

worldly pleasures wanted to see for himself the ancient texts and drink directly from the source of all wisdom. He volunteered to help copy the ancient text but soon realized that he was in fact not copying ancient texts at all. He was copying copies made by other monks who no doubt had also spent their lives copying copies of the word of God.

In his enthusiasm and curiosity, he asked the abbot if it would be possible to check the original texts, which were stored deep in the vaults of the monastery. After all, the monk reasoned if any mistakes had been made in the copies, they were now being spread from generation to generation.

The old abbot declined his request. He told the young monk not to worry about such things and the young monk dutifully obeyed.

Years later and the young monk was no longer young. Although his enthusiasm for life had become somewhat diminished over the years, his hard work and years of dutiful service had led to his being chosen as the new abbot when the old abbot had died. Now instead of filling his days copying ancient wisdom by rota, he found himself with time for contemplation and reflection. Soon his old curiosity and thirst for truth returned and he took it upon himself to go down into the vaults at the heart of the monastery.

He stayed down there for months, poring over the ancient texts by candlelight, pausing only to pray, to sleep and to eat the meals which were left outside the door of the vaults every morning.

One day, when the young monk assigned to care for him came by to gather up the empty dishes, he heard what sounded like distant crying. Although going down into the vaults was strictly forbidden, the young monk opened the door, lit a candle and made his way into the sacred heart of the monastery. There he found his beloved new abbot sobbing uncontrollably.

"What's the matter, brother?" the young monk asked the abbot.

The weary abbot looked hopelessly up into the gentle eyes of the young monk. "We've made a terrible mistake," he said. "The original word was celebrate."

153.

One person with a BELIEF

is equal to a force of ninety-nine

with only an interest.

154.

The trouble with having an open mind, of course, is that people will insist on coming along and trying to put things in it.

(Terry Pratchett)

155.

"Would you tell me please, which way I ought to go from here?"

"That depends a good deal on where you want to go."

"Oh, I don't care much where."

"Then it doesn't matter which way you go."

(Lewis Carroll, Alice in Wonderland)

156.

I'm not afraid of death; I just don't want to be there when it happens.
(Woody Allen)

157.

Nothing happens in life until you get rid of your excuses.

Get up off your ass and go make it happen.

There are no exceptions.

158.

Why Does a Bird Sing?

A teacher who had received much acclaim for his insights and discourses into the nature of the universe, was asked by one of his students about what difference he hoped to make in the world through his teachings.

After a few moments thought, the teacher replied that he had no such hopes.

"Those who can truly hear what I have to say, do not really need me to say it; those who cannot hear could listen until I was hoarse and could no longer speak without changing in the slightest."

The student was confused.

"But if you cannot make a difference with your ideas, why do you teach at all?"

The teacher smiled and replied, "Why does a bird sing?"

159.

It is in your moments of decisions that your destiny is shaped.

(Tony Robbins)

160.

You don't avoid trouble and achieving your dreams by examining every negative feeling or thought you get, and then trying to ensure those things don't happen.

That just keeps you trapped. The choice is simple; either you plan and take action to move you in the direction you want to go or you try to cope with the thoughts, feelings and experiences that threaten to overwhelm you. The first choice is called "thinking smart," and the second is called "Reaction." Either you react to life or you think and plan. As human beings we ALL have choices.

161.

When there is no enemy within,

The enemy outside can do you no harm.

(African Proverb)

162.

An Old Sioux Legend

In ancient times, the creator wanted to hide something from the humans until they were ready to see it. He gathered all the other creatures of creation to ask for their advice.

The eagle said, "Give it to me and I will take it to the highest mountain in all the land," but the creator said, "No, one day they will conquer the mountain and find it."

The salmon said, "Leave it with me and I will hide it at the very bottom of the ocean," but the creator said, "No, for humans are explorers at heart, and one day they will go there too."

The buffalo said, "I will take it and bury it in the very heart of the great plains," but the creator said, "No, for one day even the skin of the earth will be ripped open and they will find it there."

The creatures of creation were stumped, but then an old blind mole spoke up. "Why don't you put it inside them- that's the very last place they'll look.

The creator said, "It is done."

163.

You can plan your future Today;

but you can't live in your future Today.

Make the most of Today

and live every moment to the full.

164.

Relax about your future and let it go. Instead make an active commitment to enjoy this day. It is nearly impossible to accomplish anything when you're stressed out about the outcome. When you relax and become peaceful in your day, you become inspired and efficient and the future isn't something you need to worry about. WHEN your totally consumed with enjoying each day you make better choices, decisions and progress in your life. Many people cannot move on in life because they are living in the past or worried about their future. The past does not equal your future and your future is unknown, so let them both go so that you can grow. Today is all that counts; make the most of it and enjoy the process.

165.

My philosophy is that not only are you responsible for your life, but doing the best at this moment puts you in the best place for the next moment.

(Oprah Winfrey)

166.

You must develop the right psychology to succeed in life and that starts with renewing your mind.

Putting new ideas into your mind and through repetition reinforcing those ideas emotionally until they become habit, until they run automatically and become part of who you are.

167.

If you had had a perfect existence up until now, where everything had gone exactly right, you might not have a strong determination and desire to change your life. It's all of those apparently "negative things" that happen to us, which give us a huge desire to change things. That huge desire that arises within you, is like a magnetic fire and is very powerful. Be grateful for everything that caused that fire to ignite a massive desire within you, because that fire of desire will give you strength and determination, and you will change your life.

168.

The ultimate measure of a man is not where he stands in moments of comfort and convenience, but where he stands at times of challenge and controversy.

(Martin Luther King, Jr)

169.

Keep love in your heart. A life without it is like a sunless garden when the flowers are dead.

(Oscar Wilde)

170.

Your goals are the road maps that guide you and show you what is possible in your life.

(Les Brown)

171.

One way change happens is through impressions. A lot of times we know what we should do to change but we put it off, we make excuses, we reason it out. Before large changes happen in your life, you need to be satisfied with the small changes that can happen each day. Too often we put change off by thinking, "oh I don't feel like it," "I'll start on Monday," but if you don't learn to pass the small tests and get into a habit of doing what you need to do, it will ultimately keep you from the destination you want to go to. Five years later, ten years later, you end up somewhere you don't want to be and you will have a list of justification as to why you didn't get what you wanted. "It wasn't my fault," "It wasn't my time," "The economy was bad at that time," etc. You've got to take your mind off your problems and your circumstances and you have got to start focusing your mind on solutions and taking small steps to turn things around in your life.

Because whether you want to hear it or not; no matter what you are going through in your life right now, no matter how bad things may seem, you are the only one in your life that can turn it around. Other people can guide you and help you through change but you have to take responsibility for your own life and make the decision that you are the only one that can turn things around. You have to be aware how a mental diet is the key to transforming your life.

If you want to change any area of your life you have to make the necessary time to do the things that need to be done for that change to take place.

If you don't have the time to implement those changes, then things are not going to change for you and it's that simple.

If you don't make the decision to let go of the wrong things or the wrong people, then the right things and the right people will not show up.

The best life you can have is the life you create for yourself and the people around you that matter most to you. Get out there and MAKE IT HAPPEN…

You have to make that first move. It's not down to anyone else.

172.

Self-Mastery begins with mastering your thoughts;

If you don't control what goes into your mind, you can't control what you do.

Simple self-discipline enables you to condition your mind first and act afterwards.

(Napoleon Hill)

173.

Attitude

The longer I live, the more I realise the impact of attitude on life.

Attitude, to me, is more important than facts.

It is more important than the past, than education, than money, than circumstances, than failures, than successes,

than what others think or say or do.

It is more important than appearance, giftedness or skill.
It will make or break a company, a church, a home.
The remarkable thing is we have a choice everyday regarding
the attitude we will embrace for that day.

We cannot change our past. we cannot change the
fact that people will act in a certain way.
We cannot change the inevitable.

The only thing we can do is play on the one string we have, and that is our attitude. I am convinced that life is 10% what happens
to me and 90% how I react to it.
And so it is with you. We are in charge of our attitudes.

(Charles Swindoll)

174.

Whether you think you can or you think you can't,

Either way, you're right

(Henry Ford)

175.

No matter what people tell you, words and ideas can change the world.

(Robin Williams)

176.

The man who has no imagination, has no wings.

(Muhammad Ali)

177.

Everyone Has a Story in Life

A 24 year old boy seeing out from the train's window shouted,

"Dad, look the trees are going behind!"

Dad smiled and a young couple sitting nearby looked at the 24 year old's childish behaviour with pity. Suddenly he again exclaimed,

"Dad, look the clouds are running with us!"

The couple couldn't resist and said to the old man,

"Why don't you take your son to a good doctor?" The old man smiled and said, "I did and we are just coming from the hospital. My son was blind from birth, he just got his eyes today."

Every single person on the planet has a story. Don't judge people before you truly know them. The truth might surprise you.

178.

The drive to do more and achieve more separates the extraordinary from the ordinary. We all have the resources to be extraordinary. It's simply a state of mind. Whether you think you can or cannot something, either way you are right. Either way you send the suggestion to your sub-conscious mind and the appropriate actions will follow. It's amazing what you can achieve when you decide to change your mind. That's all it takes. Make a start by choosing one small thing that you have been putting off and make a decision right now to take action.

179.

Words can inspire you;

Words can destroy you.

Choose yours well.

(Robin Sharma)

180.

Do not take life too seriously. You will never get out of it alive.

(Elbert Hubbard)

181.

"I AM"- Two of the most important words-

Because what you put after them shapes your reality.

(Joel Osteen)

182.

Knowing is not enough,

We must apply.

Willing is not enough,

We Must Do

(Bruce Lee)

183.

A Dish of Ice Cream

In the days when an ice cream sundae cost much less, a ten year old boy entered a hotel coffee shop and sat at a table. A waitress put a glass of water in front of him.

"How much is an ice cream sundae.

I would really like an ice cream sundae."

"Fifty cents," replied the waitress.

The little boy pulled his hand out of his pocket and studied a number of coins in it.

"How much is a plain ice cream cone?" he inquired.

Some people were now waiting for a table and the waitress was a bit impatient.

"Thirty-five cents, can you please hurry up, I have other people waiting. I don't have all day," she said brusquely.

The little boy again counted the coins. "I'll have the plain ice cream," he said.

The waitress brought the ice cream, put the bill on the table and walked away. The boy finished the ice cream, paid the cashier and departed.

When the waitress came back, she began wiping down the table and then swallowed hard at what she saw.

There, placed neatly beside the empty dish, were fifteen cents – her tip.

(The very amount that could have got his that ice cream sundae).

184.

Daily rituals are a way of saying,

"I'm taking responsibility for my own success.

I'm steering my own ship and I will steer it with a set of revised rituals each day until that ship docks."

185.

The way you feel from moment to moment is a direct result of the way you are using particular words, pictures and images inside your mind. The worst critic you will ever encounter is the one who lives inside your own mind. But you can change your state in a moment by simply changing the way you talk to yourself and how you think and ultimately how you feel. YOU DO HAVE A CHOICE. YOU ARE IN CONTROL

186.

The universe doesn't give you what you ask for with your thoughts,

If gives you what you DEMAND with your actions.

(Dr. Steve Maraboli)

187.

With everything that has happened to you, you can either feel sorry for yourself or treat what has happened as a gift. Everything is either an opportunity to grow or an obstacle to keep you from growing. You get to choose.

(Dr. Wayne W Dyer)

188.

No matter what people tell you, words and ideas can change the world.

(Robin Williams)

189.

Procrastination is the silent killer within each of us. The secret to beating procrastination is that we need to keep motivated. Every day we must do something, anything that gets us motivated. Whether it's listening to our favourite piece of music, going for that morning walk or simply reading or listening to something that, motivates us. Every day we must motivate ourselves because when we are motivated we have energy, we have ideas and dreams and we pursue those dreams with our unbound faith that we will achieve them and more.

190.

The secret of getting ahead is getting started.

(Mark Twain)

191.

Everything you do is based on the choice you make.

It's not your parents, your past relationships, your job, the economy, the weather, an argument or your age that is to blame.

You and only you are responsible for every decision and choice you make; PERIOD.

192.

You have got to become a person of action to succeed; doing the practical things that need to be done each day that will move you in the direction of your goal. You're going to have to be prepared to start doing things you don't feel like doing to be successful.

Getting rid of procrastination and laziness in your life and having a game plan a massive action plan that you put into practice each day. Whether you like to hear it or not, being successful means getting up off your ass, not just now and again but every day and practically plugging your plan into your life. Making things happen.

The name of the game in life, if you want to become a success at anything, is results. You can always tell a person's level of awareness by the results they are getting.

193.

Stop being afraid of what could go wrong

and

start being excited about what could go right.

194.

Why do they always teach us that it's easy and evil to do what we want and that we need discipline to restrain ourselves?

It's the hardest thing in the world to do what we want. I

mean, what we really want. And it takes the greatest kind of courage."

(Ayn Rand)

195.

The only thing standing between you and your goals,

is the bullshit story you keep telling yourself.

196.

I didn't come this far,

to only come this far.

197.

The will to win, the desire to succeed, the urge to reach your full potential... these are the keys that will unlock the door to personal excellence.

(Confucius)

198.

Highly stressed people live in a highly stressed world,

Happy and contented people live in a happy and

contented world,

Same World.

199.

The Challenge

Let others lead small lives,
But not you.
Let others argue over small things,
But not you.
Let others cry over small hurts,
But not you.
Let others leave their future
In someone else's hands,
But not you.

(Jim Rohn)

200.

Success occurs when your dreams are bigger than your excuses.

201.

There are so many people out there who will tell you that you can't.

What you've got to do is turn around and say, "watch me."

202.

The Lion and the Fox

A man was walking through the woods outside his home one day when he came across a hungry fox who seemed to be at death's door. Because he was a kind man, he thought to bring it some food, but before he could go back to his home he heard a fearsome roar and hid behind a tree. In seconds, a mountain lion appeared, dragging the carcass of its freshly caught prey. The lion ate its fill and then wandered off, leaving the remains for the grateful fox.

The man was overwhelmed by this example of an abundant and benevolent universe and decided that he would not return to his home or his job. Instead of working hard to provide for himself, he would follow the example of the fox and allow the universe to provide for him.

Needless to say, the fox wandered off. As days turned to weeks the man himself was hungry and at death's door. Despite his best efforts to retain his faith, he was becoming desperate. In a rare moment of inner quiet, he heard the still, small voice of his own wisdom: "Why have you sought to emulate the fox instead of the lion?"

With that, the man returned home and ate his fill.

203.

Every day I do something better than the day before.

204.

If I was asked to give a one minute lesson on how to help a person change their life it would be this:

Start by changing what words you say to yourself on a daily basis, this then changes your thinking, which in turn changes how you feel, which will lead you to take action to achieve your goal which will build new habits. Which then sends you in a new direction in life, which ultimately will become your destiny. Summary:

WORDS=THINKING=FEELINGS=ACTIONS=HABITS=DIRECTION=DESTINY.

When you commit to this on a daily basis you can't not change. Whatever excuses you are using to stop you from changing, is committing you to staying the same. We all have a choice.

205.

I don't know where my story will end,

But nowhere in the text will it ever read,

"I gave up."

206.

The world is full of dreamers; there aren't enough who will move ahead and begin to take concrete steps to actualise their vision. Fear of failure keeps people in mediocre. There is a price to pay for everything in life. There are costs and risks to a program of action, but they are far less than the long-range risks and costs of comfortable inaction. Create a definite plan for carrying out your desire and begin at once, whether you are ready or not, to put this plan into action. Taking "consistent action" is a process to making you the person you need to be inside when you have achieved your dream.

207.

There is only one boss in life,

And that's you.

The person looking back in the mirror at you is the only one you have to answer to every day.

(Wayne Dyer)

208.

All successful people, men and women are big dreamers. They imagine what their future could be, ideal in every respect, and then they work every day toward their distant vision, that goal or purpose.

(Brian Tracy)

209.

Are you the creator of your life or a victim of circumstances? Our experiences of life, good or bad, are created from the inside, out. When you act as if your experience is created from the outside in, you will experience yourself as a victim. The minute you take responsibility for creating your experience from inside out, you reclaim your position as the creator of your life. It's your life, you create it, not anyone else. Decide to take back control as from now.

210.

The Man in The Glass

When you get what you want in your struggle for self
And the world makes you king for a day.
Just go to the mirror and look at yourself
And see what that man has to say.

For it isn't your father, or mother, or wife
Whose judgment upon you must pass.

The fellow whose verdict counts most in your life
Is the one staring back from the glass.

He's the fellow to please – never mind all the rest
For he's with you, clear to the end.
And you've passed your most difficult, dangerous test
If the man in the glass is your friend.

You may fool the whole world down the pathway of years
And get pats on the back as you pass.
But your final reward will be heartache and tears
If you've cheated the man in the glass.

(Peter Dale Wimbrow)

211.

Success depends upon previous preparation and without such preparation there is sure to be failure.

(Confucius)

212.

What stops people from daring to set big goals and taking action is the fear of failure/rejection and the limiting belief that they do not have the resources to achieve the life they want. It is very easy to feel defeated and disheartened when things don't go the way we want. It is easy to give up and think impossible, when obstacles/problems seem to make the task impossible. That is why 90% of people in life are so ordinary. They make the easy choice and quit. Remember that the winners of the world (the top 10%) face just as many obstacles/problems as everyone else. In fact, in most cases, they face even greater obstacles. The difference is that they make the tougher choice of finding a way towards their goals REGARDLESS of how impossible it seems.

213.

Impossible is a word to be found only in the dictionary of fools.

(Napoleon Bonaparte)

214.

The best preparation for tomorrow is doing your best today.

(H. Jackson Brown, Jr.)

215.

Follow Your Dream

Follow your dream.
Take one step at a time and don't settle for less,
Just continue to climb.
Follow your dream.
If you stumble, don't stop and lose sight of your goal
Press to the top.
For only on top can we see the whole view,
Can we see what we've done and what we can do;
Can we then have the vision to seek something new,
Press on.
Follow your dream.

(Amanda Bradley)

216.

The most important thing in communication is hearing what isn't said.

(Peter Drucker)

217.

Climb Til' Your Dreams Come True

Often your tasks will be many,
And more than you think you can do.
Often the road will be rugged
And the hills insurmountable, too.
But always remember,
The hills ahead
Are never as steep as they seem,
And with Faith in your heart
Start upward
And climb 'til you reach your dream.
For nothing in life that is worthy
Is ever too hard to achieve
If you have the courage to try it,
And you have the faith to believe.
For faith is a force that is greater
Than knowledge or power or skill,
And many defeats turn to triumph
If you trust in God's wisdom and will.
For faith is a mover of mountains,
There's nothing that God cannot do,
So, start out today with faith in your heart,
And climb 'til your dream comes true!

(Helen Steiner Rice)

218.

Words can hurt or heal.

What did yours do today?

219.

Throwing Starfish

A young man is walking along the ocean and sees a beach on which thousands and thousands of starfish have washed ashore. Further along he sees an old man, walking slowly and stooping often, picking up one starfish after another and tossing each one gently into the ocean. "Why are you throwing starfish into the ocean?," he asks. "Because the sun is up and the tide is going out and if I don't throw them further in they will die." "But, old man, don't you realise there is miles and miles of beach and starfish all along it! You can't possibly save them all, you can't even save one-tenth of them. In fact, even if you work all day, your efforts won't make any difference at all." The old man listened calmly and then bent down to pick up another starfish and threw it into the sea. "It made a difference to that one."

220.

If you always do what you've always done,

You'll always get what you've always got.

It's time to do something different.

(Henry Ford)

221.

Happiness is a choice.

YOU are the only person that can make you happy.

You're as happy as you choose to be.

(Rick Warren)

222.

I honestly think it is better to be a failure at something you love than to be a success at something you hate.
(George Burns)

223.

Everything you need is already within you.

The beauty of life is that your DESTINY lies always within your hands.

The time has come for you to
STEP UP and BE GREAT
(Pablo)

224.

Always bear in mind that your own resolution to succeed is more important than any other.
(Abraham Lincoln)

225.

As human beings we do not act directly on the world around us. Each of us creates a representation of the world in which we live. Our representation of the world then determines to a large degree what our experience of the world will be, how we perceive the world, what choices we will see available to us. For anyone to change a behavior that is creating a negative effect in their lives, for example, depression, fears, phobias etc., we have to change how we represent this in our minds. All negative behavior is just that, a behavior, that can easily be changed. Change happens the moment you represent the same event in your mind in a different, more empowering way.

226.

Every new day

is another chance

to change your life.

227.

The biggest mistake that you can make is to believe that you are working for somebody else. Job security is gone. The driving force of a career must come from the individual. Remember: Jobs are owned by the company; you own your career!

(Earl Nightingale)

228.

The Cookie Thief

A woman was waiting at an airport one night, with several long hours before her flight. She hunted for a book in the airport shops, bought a bag of cookies and found a place to drop.

She was engrossed in her book but happened to see, that the man sitting beside her, as bold as could be, grabbed a cookie or two from the bag in between, which she tried to ignore to avoid a scene.

So she munched the cookies and watched the clock, as the gutsy cookie thief diminished her stock. She was getting more irritated as the minutes ticked by, thinking, "if I wasn't so nice, I would blacken his eye."

With each cookie she took, he took one too. When only one was left, she wondered what he would do. With a smile on his face and a nervous laugh, he took the last cookie and broke it in half.

He offered her half as he ate the other. She snatched it from him and thought, "This guy has some nerve and he's also rude, why he didn't even show any gratitude!"

She had never known when she had been so galled, and sighed with relief when her flight was called. She gathered her belongings and headed to the gate, refusing to look back at the thieving ingrate.

She boarded the plane, and sank in her seat, then she sought her book, which was almost complete. As she reached in her baggage, she gasped with surprise, there was her bag of cookies, in front of her eyes.

"If mine are here," she moaned in despair, "the others were his and he tried to share." Too late to apologize, she realized with grief, that she was the rude one, the ingrate, the thief.

229.

If you always put limits on everything you do, physical or anything else, it will spread into your work and into your life. There are no limits. There are only plateaus, and you must not stay there, you must go beyond them.

(Bruce Lee)

230.

Where you are in life at the moment is the result of what you have been putting into your mind in the past. To change any area of your life you have to firstly go through a process of renewing your mind. Renewing the mind is a simple process of putting a new idea into your mind and through repetition reinforcing that idea until it becomes emotionally charged and becomes a habit. Changing any area of your life is not a one-time event, it's a life time endeavor. But there is a process to follow. Everybody wants to change but only a percentage of people are willing to go through the process of change. Start focusing on what you want instead of what you don't want. Where you want to go in life, instead of where you have been. What you can accomplish instead of finding fault and lack in your life. Commit to the daily actions you need to undertake to make that change go from an idea to your reality. As human beings we all have the ability to turn are lives around. It all starts with renewing your mind. What happens to you on the outside world, whether good or bad, was first created on the inside world. Think of what you would like to achieve and start developing the mindset to take you there. Renewing the mind is an exciting and powerful process.

231.

Beliefs have the power to create and the power to destroy. Human beings have the awesome ability to take any experience of their lives and create a meaning that disempowers them or one that can literally save their lives.

(Anthony Robbins)

232.

A woman's mind is cleaner than a man's; she changes it more often.

(Oliver Herford)

233.

How we feel on a daily basis is simply the result of how we manage our thoughts. Through habit we let the negative thoughts dominate our minds and the matching behavior becomes conditioned within our sub-conscious and runs on automatic. It's never the first thought or the second thought that makes you feel depressed or stressed or anxious. It's the ones your repeat over and over within your mind that lead you on a train of thought to experiencing those uncomfortable emotions. But just as you can train your mind to do one thing you can train your mind to do something else even better and more worthwhile. Instead of calling in the thought police and monitoring your negative thoughts all we need to do is simply let them pass. We have over 60,000 thoughts per day and it's the ones we get emotionally caught up in, that have meaning in our lives. When a negative thought comes into your mind and you realise, "that's just a thought," it's nothing more and simply let it pass. The simplicity of this new pattern can totally free you from the negativity you're experiencing in your mind. You're only one thought away from feeling happy, excited, joyful or even awesome. Thoughts are just thoughts, no more no less. When you start letting go of the yucky ones and realise that they are just thoughts you can direct your attention to the good ones, and through practice, how you feel from day to day changes dramatically.

234.

I believe that if life gives you lemons, you should make lemonade. And try to find somebody whose life has given them vodka and have a party.

(Ron White)

235.

There are two kinds of people in the world; those who make excuses and those who get results. An excuse person will find any excuse for why a job was not done and a results person will find any reason why it can be done. Be a creator, not a reactor.

236.

A day without sunshine is like, you know, night.

(Steve Martin)

237.

THE BUMBLEBEE

According to scientists, the bumblebee's body is too heavy and its wing span too small. Aerodynamically, the bumblebee cannot fly. But the bumblebee doesn't know that and it keeps flying.

When you don't know your limitations, you go out and surprise yourself. In hindsight, you wonder if you had any limitations. The only limitations a person has are those that are self-imposed. Don't let education put limitations on you.

238.

Go to Heaven for the climate, Hell for the company.

(Mark Twain)

239.

What is defeat?

Nothing more than education.

Nothing more than the first step to something better.

240.

It takes considerable knowledge just to realise the extent of your own ignorance.

(Thomas Sowell)

241.

Why Not You

Growing up we are told many things,
One being, you can do anything.
But somewhere between child and adult,
Things change and we no longer sing.

Life takes on a whole different meaning,
From what we may have first believed.
We all get so caught up in what life expects,
And forget what we all could achieve.

Whoever told you, you weren't allowed,
To follow all of your dreams?
Was it someone who took away your dream,
Or was it you who was afraid of your schemes?

Whatever the reason, I now must ask,
Why not you, don't you think?
It's time for you to take control of your life,
So you'll be happy to look back with no regret.

(Julie Herbert)

242.

I want my children to have all the things I couldn't afford. Then I want to move in with them.

(Phyllis Diller)

243.

When you start seeing your worth,

You'll find it hard to stay around people who don't.

244.

And thus it's always been
That question pondered down the ages
By simple men with simple ways
To wise and ancient sages.
How sweet then, quietly knowing
Reaching destination fair:
"It's the journey that's important,
Not the getting there!"

(John Leod)

245.

If you want to change your life, you can't continue to live life according to your old beliefs and attitudes. You have got to let go of the old fears and limitations that are holding you back. Just as exercise improves your health and physical fitness, a renewed mind improves your life and mental fitness. No matter what your past experiences, you have got to let the past go so that you can grow into your future. There is something amazing out there for you, you just have to go and get it. Renewing you mind is the first step. Make that crucial decision today, "it's time for change."

246.

"Success consists of going from failure to failure without loss of enthusiasm."
(Winston Churchill)

247.

Marriage is a wonderful institution, but who would want to live in an institution?

(H. L. Mencken)

248.

The first step in turning things around in your personal and business lives, is to stop complaining about how things are not working out and how difficult life is. The truth about life is this; you always get what you focus on. When you spend your time complaining and blaming everyone else about how bad things are in your life, then that's where your focus is and you tend to get more of the same. If you want more out of life then start focusing on where you want to go and get emotionally involved in those thoughts. Not only thinking about achieving the results but actually feeling how it will feel when you get there. When you get emotionally involved in your thoughts, your focus changes, not only in how you think but how you feel.

249.

If at first you don't succeed, blame your parents.

(Marcelene Cox)

250.

Taking back control of your life is about getting involved in a process. For lasting change to take place in your life 4 things MUST take place:

1. You MUST take full responsibility for your life. This means letting go of all the excuses that you are holding onto that are keeping you from being the person you want to be. It's your life, no one else's and what you allow to happen in your life is what will continue.

2. You need to forgive those who you are holding grudges against and you need to forgive yourself, letting go of any guilt you may be holding inside for things that happened in the past. The past is over, you can't change it, it has come and gone and you are only left with the memories. Reliving the memories over and over again is what keeps people contained in the emotions from the past. Have the strength and courage to forgive others and yourself.

3. You MUST go through a process of renewing your mind. Renewing your mind is a simple process of putting new ideas into you mind and through daily repetition emotionally reinforcing those ideas until they then become habit. As human beings we are emotional creatures and what you focus on daily, you feel. If you focus on how bad life is or how things have not worked out, you are going to experience the feelings associated with those thoughts. New ideas and new thoughts help you focus on something different, helping you change how you feel on a daily

basis.

4. Taking "daily action" toward your goals. You must get rid of the laziness, procrastination and excuses which means getting off your ass, not just once in a while, but every day and putting a set of daily, practical rituals into place to bring you closer in the direction of your goal. Remember you are responsible for your life, no one else, and what you allow to happen on a daily basis is what will continue.

Make a "quality decision" to start the process of turning your life around by putting these 4 simple steps into practice. You gain momentum as you go along and with a renewed mindset the people, places and things that you need will fall into place along the way.

251.

ENJOY LIFE AT EVERY MOMENT

Once a fisherman was sitting near a seashore, under the shadow of a tree smoking his pipe. Suddenly a rich businessman passing by approached him and enquired as to why he was sitting under a tree smoking and not working. To this the poor fisherman replied that he had caught enough fish for the day.

Hearing this the rich man got angry:

Businessman: "Why don't you catch more fish instead of sitting in shadow wasting your time?"

Fisherman: "What would I do by catching more fish?"

Businessman: You could catch more fish, sell them and earn more money, and buy a bigger boat.

Fisherman: What would I do then?

Businessman: You could go fishing in deep waters and catch even more fish and earn even more money.

Fisherman: What would I do then?

Businessman: You could buy many boats and employ many people to work for you and earn even more money.

Fisherman: What would I do then?

Businessman: You could become a rich businessman like me.

Fisherman: What would I do then?

Businessman: You could then enjoy your life peacefully.

Fisherman: What do you think I'm doing right now?

We don't need to wait for tomorrow to be happy and enjoy our life. We don't even need to be richer or more powerful to enjoy life.

We have all we need in the moment to be happy, enjoy it fully.

252.

Just imagine becoming the way you used to be as a very young child, before you understood the meaning of any word, before opinions took over your mind. The real you is loving, joyful, and free. The real you is just like a flower, just like the wind, just like the ocean, just like the sun.

(Don Miguel Ruiz)

253.

The trick to setting goals properly is to fully involve yourself in making things happen without investing your self-worth or emotional well-being into their achievement. Too many people get stressed when in pursuit of their goals and end up further away from them than when they started. We can only control what we are in control of. When in pursuit of your goals let go of trying to control the uncontrollable, that is, what other people will do and how things will ultimately turn out. By doing this you ironically increase your influence and the probability of getting what you want.

254.

What we think, we become.

(Buddha)

255.

Be not the slave of your own past. Plunge into the sublime seas, dive deep and swim far, so you shall come back with self-respect, with new power, with an advanced experience that shall explain and overlook the old.

(Ralph Waldo Emerson)

256.

We all make mistakes in life, that's call being human. Learning from those mistakes and moving forward builds character and prepares you for the future when your faced with similar challenges. Feeling guilty about your past mistakes and harbouring that guilt is a futile exercise. You have already paid the price for those mistakes once, you don't need to continue to pay for them over and over everyday. Let the past go. Forgive yourself and give yourself permission to face your future and live a happy, fulfilling life.

REMEMBER WHAT YOU HAVE DONE IN THE PAST HAS NOTHING TO DO WITH YOUR FUTURE.

257.

You can't depend on your eyes when your imagination is out of focus.

(Mark Twain)

258.

TEMPER CONTROL

There once was a little boy who had a bad temper. His father gave him a bag of nails and told him that every time he lost his temper, he must hammer a nail into the fence.

The first day the boy had driven 37 nails into the fence. Over the next few weeks as he learned to control his anger, the number of nails hammered daily, gradually dwindled down. He discovered it was easier to hold his temper than to drive those nails into the fence. Finally the day came when the boy didn't lose his temper at all. He told his father about it and the father suggested that the boy now pull out one nail for each day that he was able to hold his temper.

The days passed and the young boy was finally able to tell his father that all the nails were gone. The father took his son by the hand and led him to the fence. He said "you have done well, my son, but look at the holes in the fence. The fence will never be the same. When you say things in anger, they leave a scar just like this one."

You can put a knife in a man and draw it out. It won't matter how many times you say I'm sorry, the wound is still there.

Make sure you control your temper the next time you are tempted to say something you will regret later, because spoken words once out, never come back.

259.

Happiness is when what you think, what you say and what you do are in harmony.

(Mahatma Gandhi)

260.

It's The Journey That's Important

Life, sometimes so wearying
Is worth its weight in gold.
The experience of traveling
Lends a wisdom that is old.
Beyond our 'living memory'
A softly spoken prayer:
"It's the journey that's important,
Not the getting there!"

Ins and outs and ups and downs
Life's road meanders aimlessly.
Or so it seems, but somehow
Leads us where we need to be,
And being simply human
We oft question and compare.
"Is the journey so important
Or the getting there?"

262.

Courage is what it takes to stand up and speak; courage is also what it takes to sit down and listen.

(Winston Churchill)

263.

Laugh and the world laughs with you, snore and you sleep alone.

(Anthony Burgess)

264.

The Elephant Rope

As a man was passing the elephants, he suddenly stopped, confused by the fact that these huge creatures were being held by only a small rope tied to their front leg. No chains, no cages. It was obvious that the elephants could, at anytime, break away from their bonds but for some reason, they did not.

He saw a trainer nearby and asked why these animals just stood there and made no attempt to get away. "Well," the trainer said, "when they are very young and much smaller we use the same size rope to tie them and, at that age, it's enough to hold them. As they grow up, they are conditioned to believe they cannot break away. They believe the rope can still hold them, so they never try to break free."

The man was amazed. These animals could at any time break free from their bonds but because they believed they couldn't, they were stuck right where they were.

Like the elephants, how many of us go through life hanging onto a belief that we cannot do something, simply because we failed at it once before?

Failure is part of learning; we should never give up the struggle in life.

265.

The greatest achievement in life is to have the ability to create the world around you so that it matches the dreams in your head.

(Mike Dillon-Entrepreneur)

266.

The will to win, the desire to succeed, the urge to reach your full potential, these are the keys that will unlock the door to personal excellence.

(Confucius)

267.

I've missed more than 9000 shots in my career.

I've lost almost 300 games.

26 times I've been trusted to take the game winning shot and missed.

I've failed over and over and over again in my life.

And that is why I succeed.

(Michael Jordan)

268.

Man is condemned to be free; because once thrown into the world, he is responsible for everything he does.

(Jean-Paul Sartre)

269.

Value

A well known speaker started off his seminar by holding up a $20 bill. In the room of 200, he asked, "Who would like this $20 bill?"

Hands started going up.

He said, "I am going to give this $20 to one of you but first, let me do this." He proceeded to crumple the dollar bill up.

He then asked, "Who still wants it?" Still the hands were up in the air.

"Well," he replied, "What if I do this?" And he dropped it on the ground and started to grind it into the floor with his shoe.

He picked it up, now all crumpled and dirty. "Now who still wants it?" Still the hands went into the air.

"My friends, you have all learned a very valuable lesson. No matter what I did to the money, you still wanted it because it did not decrease in value. It was still worth $20. Many times in our lives, we are dropped, crumpled, and ground into the dirt by the decisions we make and the circumstances that come our way.

We feel as though we are worthless. But no matter what has happened or what will happen, you will never lose your value. You are special - Don't ever forget it!

270.

The most expensive piece of real estate is the six inches between your right and left ear. It's what you create in that area that determines your wealth. We are only really limited by our mind.

(Dolf de Roos)

271.

To effectively communicate, we must realise that we are all different in the way we perceive the world and use this understanding as a guide to our communication with others.

(Tony Robbins)

272.

Life is full of hills and valleys,

Some of which would want us to quit along the way.

It is during these times that we need to check our focus and remember that-

The focus needs to be on the finish,

Not on the difficulties along the way.

Set your eye on the goal.

Do not worry of the difficulties along the way,

Keep your focus on your goal.

273.

Success is nothing more than a few simple disciplines, practiced every day.

(Jim Rohn)

274.

Your work is going to fill a large part of your life, and the only way to be truly satisfied is to do what you believe is great work. And the only way to do great work is to love what you do. If you haven't found it yet, keep looking. Don't settle. As with all matters of the heart, you'll know when you find it.

(Steve Jobs)

275.

The discipline you learn and character you build from setting and achieving a goal can be more valuable than the achievement of the goal.

(Bo Bennett)

276.

People with goals succeed because they know where they're going.

(Earl Nightingale)

277.

No matter how talented, rich or cool, you believe that you are,

how you treat people ultimately tells all.

INTEGRITY is EVERYTHING.

278.

Procrastination is the bad habit of putting off until the day after tomorrow what should have been done the day before yesterday.

(Napoleon Hill)

279.

No one is going to stand up at your funeral and say,

She had a really expensive couch and great shoes.

Don't make life about stuff.

280.

The person we believe ourselves to be will always act in a manner consistent with our self-image.

(Brian Tracy)

281.

You can't change your life when you have an old traditional way of thinking.

Maybe you're going through some things in your life that you're struggling with and you don't know how to break those bonds and move forward.

The first key to transformation is that you've got to take your mind off yourself. You've got to take your mind of your problems and your circumstances and you have got to start focusing your mind on solutions and taking small steps to turn things around in your life. Success in life is not one event. Success in life is doing the small things each day and following through, despite the setbacks, through the challenges and whether you feel like doing it or not. This builds your character, develops your confidence and installs the new belief that you can achieve it because you have developed a brand new mindset.

No matter what you are trying to achieve; a better relationship, building a new business, learning a new skill, becoming financially independent or whatever success means to you, it is so important to develop the mindset of the person you want to become along the way. This is how the changes last and the success continues. Other people can guide you and help you through change but you have to take responsibility for your own life and make the decision that you are the only one that can turn things around. That means doing the things each day that need to be done and having the discipline to follow through. Start of a new week today-

Make this Week Count:

282.

Reality leaves a lot to the imagination.

(John Lennon)

283.

The Rich Man and the Beggar.

Many years ago, a man was sitting in quiet contemplation by a riverbank when he was disturbed by a beggar from the local village.

"Where is the stone?" the beggar demanded. "I must have the precious stone!"

The man smiled up at him, "What stone do you seek?"

"I had a dream," the beggar continued, barely able to slow his words enough to speak, "And in that dream a voice told me that if I went to the riverbank I would find a man who would give me a precious stone that would end my poverty forever!"

The man looked thoughtful then reached into his bag and pulled out a large diamond.

"I wonder if this is the stone?" he said kindly. "I found it on the path. If you like it, you may certainly have it."

The beggar couldn't believe his luck and he snatched the stone from the man's hand and ran back to the village before he could change his mind.

One year later, the beggar, now dressed in the clothes of a wealthy man, came back to the riverbank in search of his anonymous benefactor.

"You have returned, my friend!" said the man, who was again sitting in his favorite spot enjoying the peaceful flow of the water before him. "What has happened?"

The beggar humbled himself before the man.

"Many wonderful things have happened to me because of the diamond you gave me so graciously. I have become wealthy, found a wife and bought a home. I am now able to give employment to others and to do what I want, when I want, with whomever I want."

"So why have you returned?" asked the man.

"Please," the beggar said. "Teach me whatever it is inside of you that allowed you to give that stone to me."

284.

If you take responsibility for yourself, you will develop a hunger to accomplish your dreams.

(Les Brown)

285.

So I say to you, Ask and it will be given to you; search, and you will find; knock, and the door will be opened for you.

(Jesus Christ)

286.

All the great things are simple, and many can be expressed in a single word: freedom, justice, honour, duty, mercy, hope.

(Winston Churchill)

287.

Thinking "Out of the Box"

Many hundreds of years ago in a small Italian town, a merchant had the misfortune of owing a large sum of money to the moneylender. The moneylender, who was old and ugly, fancied the merchant's beautiful daughter so he proposed a bargain. He said he would forgo the merchant's debt if he could marry the daughter. Both the merchant and his daughter were horrified by the proposal.

The moneylender told them that he would put a black pebble and a white pebble into an empty bag. The girl would then have to pick one pebble from the bag. If she picked the black pebble, she would become the moneylender's wife and her father's debt would be forgiven. If she picked the white pebble she need not marry him and her father's debt would still be forgiven. But if she refused to pick a pebble, her father would be thrown into jail.

They were standing on a pebble strewn path in the merchant's garden. As they talked, the moneylender bent over to pick up two pebbles. As he picked them up, the sharp-eyed girl noticed that he had picked up two black pebbles and put them into the bag. He then asked the girl to pick her pebble from the bag.

What would you have done if you were the girl? If you had to advise her, what would you have told her? Careful analysis would produce three possibilities:

1. The girl should refuse to take a pebble.
2. The girl should show that there were two black pebbles in the bag and expose the moneylender as a cheat.
3. The girl should pick a black pebble and sacrifice herself in order to save her father from his debt and imprisonment.

The above story is used with the hope that it will make us appreciate the difference between lateral and logical thinking.

The girl put her hand into the moneybag and drew out a pebble. Without looking at it, she fumbled and let it fall onto the pebble-strewn path where it immediately became lost among all the other pebbles.

"Oh, how clumsy of me," she said. "But never mind, if you look into the bag for the one that is left, you will be able to tell which pebble I picked." Since the remaining pebble is black, it must be assumed that she had picked the white one. And since the moneylender dared not admit his dishonesty, the girl changed what seemed an impossible situation into an advantageous one.

MORAL OF THE STORY: Most complex problems do have a solution, sometimes we have to think about them in a different way.

288.

It is not how much we have, but how much we enjoy, that makes happiness.

(Charles Spurgeon)

289.

Life is really simple, but we insist on making it complicated.

(Confucius)

290.

We only get to play this game of life one time.

There's no going back to the parts we're not happy with

to do them again.

So having a game plan for the rest of your life should be just as big a part as living it.

291.

Risk comes from not knowing what you're doing.

(Warren Buffett)

292.

In order to carry a positive action we must develop here a positive vision.

(Dalai Lama)

293.

Your success in life arises from the condition of your mind

294.

Today you are you! That is truer than true! There is no one alive who is you-er than you!

(Dr. Seuss)

295.

The Value Of A Smile

The value of a smile is priceless, yet it is the cheapest, easiest, most rewarding and sincere gift to anyone that crosses your path. A smile makes a person's day, anybody's day, even a stranger's day. A smile is infectious. Start infecting people with your smile today.

A smile is nature's best antidote for discouragement. It brings rest to the weary, sunshine to those who are sad and hope to those who are hopeless and defeated.

A smile is so valuable that it can't be bought, begged, borrowed or taken away against your will. You have to be willing to give a smile away before it can do anyone else any good.

So if someone is too tired or grumpy to flash you a smile, let him have one of yours anyway. Nobody needs a smile as much as the person who has none to give.

296.

A successful man is one who makes more money than his wife can spend. A successful woman is one who can find such a man.

(Lana Turner)

297.

With each choice you make you create your life.

Believe in yourself and you will become unstoppable in whatever you set out to do. The funny thing about life is that if you refuse to accept anything but the best, you often get it. Never give up. Failure and rejection are only the first steps to succeeding.

298.

If you don't know where you are going, any road will get you there.

(Lewis Carroll)

299.

To achieve any goal in your life, you have to remove the limitations that are stopping you from getting what you want. Every limitation you have, first exists in your mind and in your thinking. If your thinking has limitations attached to it, if your mindset if limited, then your life is going to be limited. The world is full of abundance for everyone. It is only your limited thinking that stops you form achieving the life you really want.

300.

Plan your work for today and every day, then work your plan.

(Margaret Thatcher)

301.

I've come to believe that all my past failure and frustration were actually laying the foundation for the understandings that have created the new level of living I now enjoy.

(Tony Robbins)

302.

Watch your thoughts; they become words.
Watch your words; they become actions.
Watch your actions; they become habits.
Watch your habits; they become character.
Watch your character; it becomes your destiny.

(Lao-Tze)

303.

Your actions speak so loudly;

I cannot hear what you are saying

(Ralph Waldo Emerson)

304.

How we see ourselves in the privacy of our own minds determines what we will do and what will not attempt to do in life. Our "sub-conscious self-image" is that little picture we have of ourselves, that we carry around within us every minute of the day. This picture dictates how we choose to live our lives. If we have a bad picture then it stops us from stretching ourselves and opening up to our true potential and abilities. But here's the truth; that picture is not real. We make it up through our imagination and then reinforce it until it becomes our reality(even though it's not reality in actuality) and then we act out on it as if it's real. We put labels on ourselves such as, low self-esteem, no confidence, withdrawn, shy etc, but all the while, we are making it up through our imagination. The truth is that at any time in your life, no matter how long you have been carrying around this false perception of yourself, you can decide to stop doing something that is not working and decide to do something different and even better. If we are making stuff up then we can decide to make up something different up; change the picture of how we see ourselves, get rid of the label attached to that old picture and create something empowering that will bring you a happier, healthier and more content life. Our imagination is so powerful and if we learn how to use it properly, our world on the outside changes because we change our inside world. You have been making things up in your imagination for years so you don't need to learn how to do it, just start shifting your focus of how you see yourself. Decide what you would like that picture of yourself to be and imagine what it would be like to be that kind of person. Start reinforcing that new imagine through repetition into your sub-conscious mind and then start acting out on that new perception of yourself as if it's real. Start with small things and build your confidence in yourself. If you can do something one way then you can do it in reverse. Once you start changing how you see yourself inside your mind, it's amazing how many opportunities start coming your way, how many things you can do when before you didn't think you could and how kinder you are to yourself when you have a new self image. Remember we make it all up, so start making up something different, something more empowering that strengthens who you are as a person inside. You can't always control your circumstances but you can always change how you see yourself in those circumstances and that starts by changing that simple picture inside your mind- YOUR SUB-CONSCIOUS SELF IMAGE and acting out on that new reality.

305.

We must develop and maintain the capacity to forgive. He who is devoid of the power to forgive is devoid of the power to love. There is some good in the worst of us and some evil in the best of us. When we discover this, we are less prone to hate our enemies.

(Martin Luther King, Jr.)

306.

STORY OF A BLIND GIRL

There was a blind girl who hated herself just because she was blind. She hated everyone, except her loving boyfriend. He was always there for her. She said that if she could only see the world, she would marry her boyfriend.

One day, someone donated a pair of eyes to her and then she could see everything, including her boyfriend. Her boyfriend asked her, "now that you can see the world, will you marry me?"

The girl was shocked when she saw that her boyfriend

was blind too, and refused to marry him. Her boyfriend walked away in tears, and later wrote a letter to her saying:

"Just take care of my eyes dear."

This is how the human brain changes when the status changed. Only a few remember what life was before, and who's always been there even in the most painful situations.

307.

Fantasy is a necessary ingredient in living, it's a way of looking at life through the wrong end of a telescope, and that enables you to laugh at life's realities.

(Dr. Seuss)

308.

It does not matter how slowly you go as long as you do not stop.

(Confucius)

309.

Where you are in life right now at this present time is no one else's fault. You are where you are because of the decisions and the choices you have made in the past.

Where you will end up in 5 years and 10 years' time will depend on the decisions and the choices you make right now at this stage of your life. There are 3 fundamental principles that are universal to anyone that will help them take back control of their lives and get back on track. Those 3 fundamental principles are:

1. You must take responsibility for your own life: Stop blaming your past, your circumstances and other people for where you are. When you make the decision to take responsibility for your life, you also make the decision to take back control of your life.

2. You must re-new your mind on a regular basis: Moving in a new direction in life is like learning a new skill. Retraining your mind with new thoughts, new ideas, developing new beliefs and gaining unstoppable confidence in yourself so that you are developing the person you need to become mentally, on your way to your goal.

3. Putting on your own C.A. P: You need a Continuous Action Plan: nothing happens without taking action and consistent action on a daily basis.

No matter who you are or where you are from in the world, if you simply made a true decision to change and start by following these 3 simply principles, you will be amazed at how quickly your life will start to move in a different direction.

310.

The possession of anything begins in the mind.
(Bruce Lee)

311.

"Whether you think you can, or you think you can't – you're right."

(Henry Ford)

312.

"If you can dream it, then you can achieve it. You will get all you want in life if you help enough other people get what they want."

(Zig Ziglar)

313.

However difficult life may seem, there is always something you can do and succeed at.

(Stephen Hawking)

314.

It is the mind that maketh good or ill,

That maketh wretch or happy, rich or poor.

(Edmund Spenser)

315.

"Imperfection is beauty, madness is genius and it's better to be absolutely ridiculous than absolutely boring."
(Marilyn Monroe)

316.

The mind is its own place, and in itself can make a

Heav'n of Hell, a Hell of Heav'n.

(John Milton)

317.

Don't find fault, find a remedy.

(Henry Ford)

318.

"Begin at the beginning," the king said gravely,

"And go till you come to the end; then stop"

(Alice's Adventures in Wonderland, Lewis Carroll)

319.

Each morning when I open my eyes I say to myself: I, not events, have the power to make me happy or unhappy today. I can choose which it shall be. Yesterday is dead, tomorrow hasn't arrived yet. I have just one day, today, and I'm going to be happy in it.

(Groucho Marx)

320.

We need to internalise this idea of excellence. Not many folks spend a lot of time trying to be excellent.

(Barack Obama)

321.

Accept responsibility for your life. Know that it is you who will get you where you want to go, no one else.

(Les Brown)

322.

Get going. Move forward. Aim high. Plan a takeoff. Don't just sit on the runway and hope someone will come along and push the airplane. It simply won't happen. Change your attitude and gain some altitude. Believe me, you'll love it up here.

(Donald J. Trump)

323.

People who think they know everything are a great annoyance to those of us who do.

(Isaac Asimov)

323.

How do you become successful;

Become so good at what you do, they can't ignore you.

(Steve Martin)

324.

Psychology is simply a mindset. Having an extraordinary psychology is simply knowing what you want from your life and living life on your terms. You decide what will give you the greatest quality of life; not your boss, not your friends, not what you have read in the latest fashion magazine. What do you really want for your life? What is going to give you fulfilment? Not success on somebody else's terms. Success without fulfilment is ultimate failure. Decide what you want and turn it into a must. Ask yourself the question, "What do I really want for my life?" Reignite that passion and then ask yourself, " What would I do if I new I couldn't fail?" By simply asking yourself new questions you send your subconscious mind in a new direction. Remember it's your mind, it's there to give you what you want, you just have to set the direction.

325.

It's simple, if it jiggles, it's fat.

(Arnold Schwarzenegger)

326.

"When one door of happiness closes, another opens; but often we look so long at the closed door that we do not see the one which has been opened for us."
(Unknown)

327.

I believe that everything happens for a reason. People change so that you can learn to let go, things go wrong so that you appreciate them when they're right, you believe lies so you eventually learn to trust no one but yourself, and sometimes good things fall apart so better things can fall together.

(Marilyn Monroe)

328.

Since your emotions are a direct response of your thoughts, logic suggests that the only thing that will change them is to change your thoughts. Yet our thoughts are simply internal conversations and mental movies which have no power to impact our lives until we charge them up by deciding they are important and real. That's why the important thing to realise about your thinking, particularly your "unhappy thinking," is that it's almost never the first thought that hurts, it's the fifth or fiftieth or even the hundredth, which inevitably comes when you follow a negative train of thoughts to a destination you don't want to go. So it's not the thoughts that pass through your head, but the ones you take ownership of and meditate on over a period of time. When we get "hooked by a thought" we give our attention to that train of thoughts and the thought becomes more real to us over time and has more and more power over our life. Accept your life for who you are and what you have. When you take that approach you are saying to yourself "I have the serenity to accept the things I cannot control, the strength to change the things I can, and the wisdom to know the difference". You'll be amazed how much more peaceful your life becomes and you start making better decisions about your future.

329.

All you can change is yourself, but sometimes that changes everything!

(Gary W Goldstein)

330.

Success is falling nine times and getting up ten.

(Jon Bon Jovi)

331.

Why, sometimes I've believed as many as six impossible things before breakfast.

(Lewis Carroll)

332.

We are at our very best, and we are happiest, when we are fully engaged in work we enjoy on the journey toward the goal we've established for ourselves. It gives meaning to our time off and comfort to our sleep. It makes everything else in life so wonderful, so worthwhile.

(Earl Nightingale)

333.

We must all suffer one of two things; the pain of discipline or the pain of regret or disappointment.

(Jim Rohn)

334.

I believe in rules. Sure I do. If there weren't any rules, how could you break them?

(Leo Durocher)

335.

Greatness is not measured by what a man or woman accomplishes, but by the opposition he or she has overcome to reach his goals.

(Dorothy Height)

336.

The 'self-image' is the key to human personality and human behavior. Change the self-image and you change the personality and the behavior.

(Maxwell Maltz)

337.

I've been lucky. Opportunities don't often come along. So, when they do, you have to grab them.

(Audrey Hepburn)

338.

Where do we enrol in Life 101? Where are the classes dealing with the loss of a job, the death of a loved one, the failure of a relationship? Unfortunately, those lessons are mostly learned through trial by fire and the school of hard knocks.

(Les Brown)

339.

We need to find God, and he cannot be found in noise and restlessness. God is the friend of silence. See how nature - trees, flowers, grass- grows in silence; see the stars, the moon and the sun, how they move in silence. We need silence to be able to touch souls.

(Mother Teresa)

340.

You have brains in your head. You have feet in your shoes. You can steer yourself in any direction you choose. You're on your own, and you know what you know. And you are the guy who'll decide where to go.

(Dr. Seuss)

341.

It is easy to hate and it is difficult to love. This is how the whole scheme of things works. All good things are difficult to achieve; and bad things are very easy to get.

(Confucius)

342.

SPEND TIME WITH YOUR FAMILY

A man narrating his date with his mother after 21 years.

After 21 years of marriage, my wife wanted me to take

another woman out to dinner and a movie. She said, "I love you, but I know this other woman loves you and would love to spend some time with you."

The other woman that my wife wanted me to visit was my MOTHER, who has been a widow for 19 years, but the demands of my work and my three children had made it possible to visit her only occasionally. That night I called to invite her to go out for dinner and a movie. "What's wrong, are you well?" she asked.

My mother is the type of woman who suspects that a late night call or a surprise invitation is a sign of bad news. "I thought that it would be pleasant to spend some time with you," I responded. "Just the two of us." She thought about it for a moment, and then said, "I would like that very much."

That Friday after work, as I drove over to pick her up I was a bit nervous. When I arrived at her house, I noticed that she too, seemed to be nervous about our date. She waited in the door with her coat on. She had curled her hair and was wearing the dress that she had worn to celebrate her last wedding anniversary. She smiled from a face that was as radiant as an angel's. "I told my friends that I was going to go out with my son, and they were impressed," she said, as she got into the car. "They can't wait to hear about our meeting."

We went to a restaurant that, although not elegant, was

very nice and cozy. My mother took my arm as if she were the First Lady. After we sat down, I had to read the menu. Her eyes could only read <u>large print</u>. Half way through the entries, I lifted my eyes and saw Mom sitting there staring at me. A nostalgic smile was on her lips. "It was I who used to have to read the menu when you were small," she said. "Then it's time that you relax and let me return the favour," I responded. During the dinner, we had an agreeable conversation – nothing extraordinary but catching up on recent events of each other's life. We talked so much that we missed the movie. As we arrived at her house later, she said, "I'll go out with you again, but only if you let me invite you." I agreed.

"How was your dinner date?" asked my wife when I got home. "Very nice. Much more so than I could have imagined," I answered.

A few days later, my mother died of a massive heart attack. It happened so suddenly that I didn't have a chance to do anything for her. Sometime later, I received an envelope with a copy of a restaurant receipt from the same place mother and I had dined. An attached note said: "I paid this bill in advance. I wasn't sure that I could be there; but nevertheless, I paid for two plates – one for you and the other for your wife. You will never know what that night meant for me. I love you, son."

At that moment, I understood the importance of saying

in time: "I LOVE YOU" and to give our loved ones the time that they deserve.

Nothing in life is more important than your family. Give them the time they deserve, because these things cannot be put off till some other time.

343.

If you don't design your own life plan, chances are you'll fall into someone else's plan. And guess what they have planned for you? Not much.

(Jim Rohn)

344.

"But I don't want to go among mad people," said Alice. "Oh, you can't help that," said the cat. "We're all mad here."

(Lewis Carroll)

345.

Never, never, never give up.

(Winston Churchill)

346.

g man asked Socrates the secret to success. ...es told the young man to meet him near the river the next morning. They met. Socrates asked the young man to walk with him toward the river. When the water got up to their neck, Socrates took the young man by surprise and ducked him into the water. The boy struggled to get out but Socrates was strong and kept him there until the boy started turning blue.

Socrates pulled his head out of the water and the first thing the young man did was to gasp and take a deep breath of air. Socrates asked, " What did you want the most when you were there?" The boy replied, "Air." Socrates said: "That is the secret to success. When you want success as badly as you wanted the air, then you will get it. There is no other secret."

347.

Strive not to be a success, but rather to be of value.

(Albert Einstein)

348.

I attribute my success to this: I never gave or took any excuse.

(Florence Nightingale)

349.

You miss 100% of the shots you don't take.

(Wayne Gretzky)

350.

Definiteness of purpose is the starting point of all achievement.

(W. Clement Stone)

351.

Life is 10% what happens to me and 90% of how I react to it.

(Charles Swindoll)

352.

The best time to plant a tree was 20 years ago. The second best time is now.

(Chinese Proverb)

353.

Every child is an artist. The problem is how to remain an artist once he grows up.

(Pablo Picasso)

354.

Either you run the day, or the day runs you.

(Jim Rohn)

355.

Try not to become a man of success, but rather try to become a man of value.

(Albert Einstein)

356.

Puppies For Sale

A store owner was tacking a sign above his door that read "Puppies For Sale." Signs like that have a way of attracting small children, and sure enough, a little boy appeared under the store owner's sign. "How much are you going to sell the puppies for?" he asked.

The store owner replied, "Anywhere from $30 to $50."

The little boy reached in his pocket and pulled out some change. "I have $2.37," he said. "Can I please look at them?"

The store owner smiled and whistled and out of the kennel came Lady, who ran down the aisle of his store followed by five teeny, tiny balls of fur.

One puppy was lagging considerably behind. Immediately the little boy singled out the lagging, limping puppy and said, "What's wrong with that little dog?"

The store owner explained that the veterinarian had examined the little puppy and had discovered it didn't have a hip socket. It would always limp. It would always be lame.

The little boy became excited. "That is the puppy that I want to buy."

The store owner said, "No, you don't want to buy that little dog. If you really want him, I'll just give him to you."

The little boy got quite upset. He looked straight into the store owner's eyes, pointing his finger, and said, "I don't want you to give him to me. That little dog is worth every bit as much as all the other dogs and I'll pay full price. In fact, I'll give you $2.37 now, and 50 cents a month until I have him paid for."

The store owner countered, "You really don't want to buy this little dog. He is never going to be able to run and jump and play with you like the other puppies."

To his surprise, the little boy reached down and rolled up his pant leg to reveal a badly twisted, crippled left leg supported by a big metal brace. He looked up at the store owner and softly replied, "Well, I don't run so well myself, and the little puppy will need someone who understands!"

What we all need is someone who understands us!!!

357.

We all need people who will give us feedback. That's how we improve.

(Bill Gates)

358.

Be yourself; everyone else is already taken.

(Oscar Wilde)

359.

If you want to know what a man's like, take a good look at how he treats his inferiors, not his equals.
(Harry Potter and the Goblet of Fire, J.K. Rowling)

360.

Always forgive your enemies; nothing annoys them so much.

(Oscar Wilde)

361.

Here's to the crazy ones. The misfits. The rebels. The troublemakers. The round pegs in the square holes. The ones who see things differently. They're not fond of rules. And they have no respect for the status quo. You can quote them, disagree with them, glorify or vilify them. About the only thing you can't do is ignore them. Because they change things. They push the human race forward. And while some may see them as the crazy ones, we see genius. Because the people who are crazy enough to think they can change the world, are the ones who do.

(Rob Siltanen)

362.

When you going through hell;

Just keep going

(Winston Churchill)

363.

It is better to be hated for what you are than to be loved for what you are not.

(André Gide, Autumn Leaves)

364.

Forgive yourself for your faults and your mistakes and move on.

(Les Brown)

365.

"The Paradoxical Commandments

People are illogical, unreasonable, and self-centred.
Love them anyway.

If you do good, people will accuse you of selfish ulterior motives.
Do good anyway.

If you are successful, you will win false friends and true enemies.
Succeed anyway.

The good you do today will be forgotten tomorrow.
Do good anyway.

Honesty and frankness make you vulnerable.
Be honest and frank anyway.

The biggest men and women with the biggest ideas can be shot down by the smallest men and women with the smallest minds.

Think big anyway.

People favor underdogs but follow only top dogs.
Fight for a few underdogs anyway.

What you spend years building may be destroyed overnight.
Build anyway.

People really need help but may attack you if you do help them.
Help people anyway.

Give the world the best you have and you'll get kicked in the teeth.

Give the world the best you have anyway."

(The Silent Revolution, Kent M. Keith)

Author's Note

I hope you enjoyed reading through the content of my latest book.

It's always a great pleasure to know that I am helping someone, whether it be in person, through my private practice or in the content from my books.

At the start of 2016 I set myself a goal to write and publish ten books within three years, all with the theme of helping people improve the quality of their lives. This read is the second book of that goal.

My first book "The Success Habit: A Journey to Self-Mastery" is a basis step by step guide to self-improvement, so if you haven't read it I would highly recommend it, as I have received so much feedback from clients and readers reinforcing the simplicity of it's message and how it has changed their lives.

Sometimes when we want to change something in our lives, we over complicate things when most of the time all it takes is a simple shift in your thinking and then approaching life's challenges one step at a time. My first book will help you achieve that goal.

So for now I want to wish you every success in your future, no matter what success means to you and I hope you will watch out for this author's name again. I promise to bring some great content in the future that can help you improve the way you live your life by developing your mindset.

So, take care for now and God Bless,

Robert

Printed in Poland
by Amazon Fulfillment
Poland Sp. z o.o., Wrocław